GUINNESS WORLD RECORDS 2016
BLOCK BUSTERS!

OFFICIALLY AMAZING

British Library
Cataloguing-in-publication data: a catalogue record for this book is available from the British Library.

ISBN
10: 1-910561-22-3
13: 978-1-910561-22-5

Records are made to be broken—indeed, it is one of the key criteria for a record category—so if you find a record that you think you can beat, tell us about it by making a record claim. Find out how on pp. 6–7. Always contact us before making a record attempt.

Guinness World Records does not claim to own any right, title, or interest in any third party intellectual property reproduced in this book. For picture credits, please refer to page 214.

Check the official website—**www.guinnessworldrecords.com**—regularly for record-breaking news, plus video footage of record attempts. You can also join and interact with the Guinness World Records online community.

Sustainability
The paper used for this edition is manufactured by UPM Plattling, Germany. The production site has forest certification and its operations have both ISO14001 environmental management system and EMAS certification to ensure sustainable production.

UPM Papers are true Biofore products, produced from renewable and recyclable materials.

© 2016 Guinness World Records Limited, a Jim Pattison Group company

BLOCKBUSTERS 2016

PROJECT EDITOR
Adam Millward

EDITOR-IN-CHIEF
Craig Glenday

SENIOR MANAGING EDITOR
Stephen Fall

GAMING EDITOR
Stephen Daultrey

PROOFREADER
Matthew White

AMERICANIZER
Theresa Bebbington

INDEXER
Marie Lorimer

PICTURE EDITOR
Michael Whitty

DEPUTY PICTURE EDITOR
Fran Morales

PICTURE RESEARCHER
Laura Nieberg

TALENT RESEARCHER
Jenny Langridge

ORIGINAL PHOTOGRAPHY
Sonja Horsman

VP PUBLISHING
Jenny Heller

DIRECTOR OF PROCUREMENT
Patricia Magill

PUBLISHING MANAGER
Jane Boatfield

PRODUCTION ASSISTANT
Thomas McCurdy

PRODUCTION CONSULTANTS
Roger Hawkins, Dennis Thon

PRINTING & BINDING
MOHN Media Mohndruck GmbH, Gütersloh, Germany

DESIGN
Neal Cobourne, Nick Evans, Sue Michniewicz, Paul Oakley

REPROGRAPHICS
Res Kahraman, Born Group

CONTRIBUTORS
Mark Aston, Rohan Mehra, Matthew White, Robert Zwetsloot

GUINNESS WORLD RECORDS

CORPORATE OFFICE
Global President: Alistair Richards

PROFESSIONAL SERVICES
Chief Financial Officer: Alison Ozanne
Financial Controller: Zuzana Reid
Management Accountants: Shabana Zaffar, Daniel Ralph
Account Receivable Manager: Lisa Gibbs
Assistant Accountant: Jess Blake
Accounts Payable Manager: Victoria Aweh
Trading Analysis Manager: Andrew Wood
Head of Legal & Business Affairs: Raymond Marshall/Kate Taylor
Solicitor: Terence Tsang
Legal & Business Affairs Executive: Xiangyun Rablen
Office Manager: Jackie Angus
Director of IT: Rob Howe
Development IT Manager: James Edwards
Desktop Administrator: Ainul Ahmed
Developer: Cenk Selim
Junior Developer: Lewis Ayers
Head of HR: Farrella Ryan-Coker

RECORDS MANAGEMENT TEAM
SVP Records: Marco Frigatti
Head of RMT Operations: Jacqui Sherlock
Records Managers: Corrinne Burns, Sam Golin, Christopher Lynch, Sam Mason, Mark McKinley, Victoria Tweedy, Aleksandr Vypirailenko
Information & Research Manager: Carim Valerio
Adjudications Manager: Ben Backhouse
Specialist Records Manager: Anatole Baboukhian
Customer Service Managers: Louise McLaren/Janet Craffey
Senior Project Manager: Alan Pixsley

Attractions Development Manager: Louise Toms
Project Manager: Shantha Chinniah
Records Consultant: Sophie Molloy
Official Adjudicators: Jack Brockbank, Fortuna Burke, Evelyn Carrera, Kimberley Dennis, Brittany Dunn, Michael Empric, John Garland, Şeyda Subaşı Gemici, Sofia Greenacre, Mai McMillan, Eva Norroy, Anna Orford, Pravin Patel, Justin Patterson, Glenn Pollard, Philip Robertson, Lucia Sinigagliesi, Lorenzo Veltri

GLOBAL BRAND STRATEGY
SVP Global Brand Strategy: Samantha Fay

GLOBAL PRODUCT MARKETING
VP Global Product Marketing: Katie Forde
B2B Product Marketing Manager: Tanya Batra
Digital Product Marketing Manager: Veronica Irons
Online Editor: Kevin Lynch
Community Manager: Dan Thorne
Digital Video Producer: Matt Musson
Designer: Jon Addison
Junior Designer: Rebecca Buchanan Smith
Product Marketing Assistant: Victor Fenes

TV & PROGRAMMING
Director of Global TV Content & Sales: Rob Molloy
Senior TV Distribution Manager: Paul Glynn
Senior TV Content Executive: Jonathon Whitton

EMEA & APAC
SVP EMEA & APAC: Nadine Causey
VP Creative: Paul O'Neill
PR Director: Amarilis Whitty

PR Managers: Doug Male, Melanie DeFries
Senior Publicist: Madalyn Bielfeld
UK & International Press Officer: Jamie Clarke
Head of Marketing: Justine Tommey
B2B Marketing Manager: Mawa Rodriguez
B2C Marketing Executive: Christelle BeTrong
Head of Publishing Sales: John Pilley
Sales & Distribution Manager: Richard Stenning
Licensing Manager, Publishing: Emma Davies
Head of Commercial Sales: Sam Prosser
Commercial Account Managers: Lucie Pessereau, Roman Sosnovsky, Jessica Rae, Inga Ramussen
Commercial Account Executives: Sadie Smith, Fay Edwards
Commercial Representative, India: Nikhil Shukla
Country Manager, MENA: Talal Omar
Project Manager: Samer Khallouf
B2B Marketing Manager: Leila Issa
Commercial Account Manager: Muhsen Jalal

AMERICAS
SVP Americas: Peter Harper
Publishing Sales & Product Director: Jennifer Gilmour
Head of Client Services: Amanda Mochan
Director of RMT—Latin America: Carlos Martinez
Head of RMT—North America: Kimberly Partrick
Account Managers: Nicole Pando, Alex Angert
Commercial Representative, Latin America: Ralph Hannah
Junior Account Manager: Hanna Kubat
PR Manager: Kristen Ott

B2B Marketing Executive: Tavia Levy
Project Manager: Casey DeSantis
Records Managers: Raquel Assis, Michael Furnari
HR & Office Manager: Kellie Ferrick

JAPAN
VP Japan: Erika Ogawa
Office Manager: Fumiko Kitagawa
Director of RMT: Kaoru Ishikawa
Project Manager: Aya McMillan
Records Managers: Mariko Koike, Gulnaz Ukassova
Designer: Momoko Cunneen
Senior PR Manager & Sales Promotion: Kazami Kamioka
Digital & Publishing Content Manager: Takafumi Suzuki
Commercial Sales & Marketing Director: Vihag Kulshrestha
Marketing Executive: Asumi Funatsu
Account Manager: Takuro Maruyama
Senior Account Executive: Daisuke Katayama
Account Executive: Minami Ito

GREATER CHINA
President: Rowan Simons
HR & Office Manager: Tina Shi
Office Assistant: Kate Wang
Marketing Director: Sharon Yang
Digital Business Manager: Jacky Yuan
B2B Marketing Manager: Iris Hou
Marketing Executive: Tracy Cui
PR Executive: Leila Wang
Head of RMT: Charles Wharton
Records Managers: Lisa Hoffman, Alicia Zhao
Records Manager/Project Coordinator: Fay Jiang
Content Director: Angela Wu
Commercial Director: Blythe Fitzwilliam
Senior Account Managers: Dong Cheng, Catherine Gao, Lessi Li
Account Manager: Chloe Liu

OFFICIALLY AMAZING

THE JIM PATTISON GROUP

GUINNESS WORLD RECORDS 2016 BLOCKBUSTERS!

CONTENTS

INTRODUCTION

Welcome to the first ever edition of *Blockbusters!*—an exciting new book from Guinness World Records. From the biggest movie releases and chart-topping music acts to the most popular apps, and the rising superstars of social media—we're looking at you, PewDiePie—this is a record-focused snapshot of the year's hottest property.

Beyond showbiz and media, we also turn the GWR spotlight on what's been trending in toys and technology, so ready yourself for more LEGO®, drones, and wearable gadgets than you can shake a selfie stick at. So without further ado, it's time to rollout the red carpet for some of the year's most high-profile record-breakers.

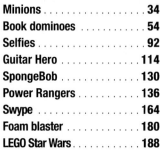

Records that will make you say "Wow!"

HOW TO BE A RECORD-BREAKER

You don't just have to read about the amazing achievements of your favorite stars and franchises—you can get involved in the blockbusting action yourself! Throughout the book, you'll find a range of specially chosen GWR challenges that offer you the chance to set your very own records—just keep an eye out for the stopwatch logo. Opposite are a few basic steps, but more specific guidelines are included on each challenge. So what are you waiting for? On your marks, get set, go!

ARE YOU UP FOR THE CHALLENGE?

Discover A-list celebs' latest achievements

Cool top 10 lists round off each chapter

Bonus facts and trivia throughout

The secrets behind mega collections in exclusive Q & As

Incredible stats that will blow your mind

Showstopping photographs

1 Go to **www.guinnessworld records.com/blockbusters** to check out the full guidelines so that you know exactly what the record attempt involves and what equipment you will need. Make sure preapproved items are signed off by GWR.

2 On the day of the challenge, keep the guidelines close on hand to use as a checklist to make sure that no rules are overlooked. Get someone who is experienced with a video camera to record the full attempt as evidence.

3 Submit all your evidence for assessment, then sit back and wait to hear whether you've become a Blockbuster!

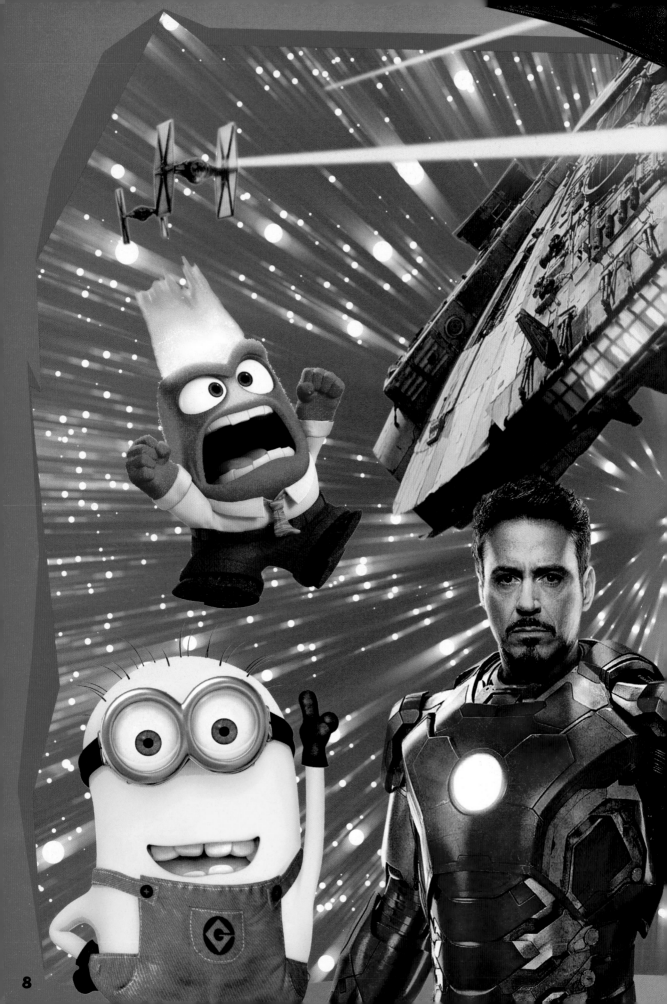

MOVIES

MOVIES

BOX-OFFICE BLOCKBUSTERS

HIGHEST-GROSSING ...

COMEDY-SPY MOVIE

Minions have taken over the planet in recent years. Their most successful movie-theater outing to date is *Despicable Me 2* (2013), which took $974,873,764 worldwide, though 2015 spin-off *Minions* is close behind on $961,293,126 at the time of going to press. If you're a fan of the yella fellas, be sure to check out our Minion-inspired challenge on pp. 34–35!

WOW!

UNDERWATER MOVIE

Considering that more than 70 percent of Earth is covered by sea, it's no surprise that so many movies focus on what may be going on below the waves. As far as ocean odysseys go, Pixar's *Finding Nemo* hit the jackpot in 2003. The plot follows hapless clownfish (*Amphiprion ocellaris*) Marlin, who during the quest for his missing son makes a few fishy friends and enemies. The *fin*-tastic film grossed $936,429,370.

PUPPET MOVIE

From Miss Piggy and Kermit the Frog (above) to Rizzo the Rat and Fozzie Bear, the Muppets have been household names across generations. Although their roots lie in television—along with their *Sesame Street* pals (pp. 140–41)—they have also been on several big-screen adventures, too. None has been more profitable than their 2011 Disney revamp, *The Muppets*, which took $160,971,922 globally. Surely these peppy puppets deserve a hand for that!

ANIMATED ROBOT MOVIE

Baymax, the star of *Big Hero 6*, is not your typical robot (he's inflatable). Neither is he your typical hero (again, he's inflatable). Nevertheless, his friendship with human companion Hiro and their battle against an evil professor and an army of microbots took movie theaters by storm in 2015, pulling in $652,127,828. This means that *Big Hero 6* outdid the 2008 animated robot flick *WALL•E* by more than $119 million!

CHRISTMAS MOVIE

A lot of popular movies are set around the festive season, but in terms of films *about* Christmas, none has earned more at the box office than 2000's *How the Grinch Stole Christmas*, with a gross of $345,141,403. Starring Jim Carrey as the Noël-hating monster, the story is based on the illustrated book by American writer and cartoonist Theodor "Dr. Seuss" Geisel. Dr. Seuss' *The Cat in the Hat* also got a live-action adaptation, in 2003.

DRAGON MOVIE

… and it's not *How to Train Your Dragon*, because the second installment of J. R. R. Tolkien's *Hobbit* trilogy was on a whole other (dragon) scale. *The Desolation of Smaug* (2013) took a huge bite of the year's Christmas box-office takings: $960,366,855. Part one, *An Unexpected Journey* (2012), grossed more—at least a billion—but only briefly featured Smaug at the end, so doesn't qualify as a "dragon movie."

MOVIES

FROZEN

THE ICE-COOL RECORD-BRRRRREAKER

HIGHEST-GROSSING MOVIE BY A FEMALE DIRECTOR

Most of the Hollywood bigwigs are men, but *Frozen* was cowritten and codirected by Jennifer Lee (USA). This makes *Frozen* the most successful film directed by a woman. The movie went on to become a billion-dollar blockbuster, so it's also the **first movie directed by a woman to earn $1 billion at the box office**.

MOST LANGUAGES FEATURED ON A SINGLE (MULTIPLE SINGERS)

"Let It Go" is the hit song that Queen Elsa sings, voiced by Idina Menzel. As well as the normal song that you hear in the movie, there's a version that's sung in a record-breaking 25 different languages by 22 different female vocalists. The lyrics are performed in English, French, German, Dutch, Polish, Mandarin, Swedish, Japanese, Latin American Spanish, Hungarian, Castilian Spanish, Catalan, Italian, Korean, Serbian, Cantonese, Portuguese, Bahasa Malaysia, Russian, Danish, Bulgarian, Norwegian, Thai, Canadian French, and Flemish.

IDINA MENZEL SINGING "LET IT GO" AT THE OSCARS

WOW!

HIGHEST-GROSSING ANIMATED MOVIE

Frozen was inspired by *The Snow Queen*—a fairy tale written by Hans Christian Andersen. The movie was released by Disney in November 2013, and by June 5, 2015, had earned an astonishing $1,274,234,980 at the worldwide box office. It's now the seventh most successful movie of all time!

MOST PIRATED ANIMATED MOVIE

In 2014, *Frozen* set another world record—and probably one that the producers were not very happy about. According to the movie-piracy experts Excipio, the movie was downloaded illegally 29.919 million times. This is equal to ticket sales of nearly $240 million.

420,000 STRANDS OF CGI HAIR on Elsa's head (largely made up of her braid). This is compared with 27,000 strands used for Rapunzel in *Tangled*.

TOP 5 DISNEY MOVIES

1. *Frozen*
$1,274,234,980

2. *Big Hero 6*
$652,127,828

3. *Tangled*
$586,581,936

4. *Wreck-It Ralph*
$473,412,677

5. *Bolt*
$328,015,209

Source: The Numbers (September 2015)

MOVIES

FROZEN

WANNA BUILD A (REALLY BIG) SNOWMAN?

MOST SNOWMEN BUILT IN ONE HOUR

People love snowmen! A total of 1,279 snowmen were made by Clearlink (USA, above) on the 18th fairway of the Mountain Dell Golf Course in Salt Lake City, Utah, on January 15, 2011. Then on February 15, 2015, the Iiyama Snow Festival (Japan) beat this with 1,585 snowmen in Nagano, Japan. Just a few days later, on February 28, 2015, the record was smashed by the creators of the Japanese TV show *Unhandy Handyman*, who made 2,036 snowmen in Hokkaido (inset). Brrrrrilliant!

LARGEST COLLECTION OF SNOWMEN

It's like Christmas every day in Coon Rapids, Minnesota! Here, snowman fan Karen Schmidt (USA) shares her home with 5,127 snowmen, which she's been collecting for more than 30 years. Luckily for the snowmen—and Karen's carpets—they're not made of snow … they're all stuffed toys, ornaments, and ceramics.

FASTEST MARATHON DRESSED AS A SNOWMAN

On your marks … get set … snow! While most snowmen are frozen to the spot, this one ran a marathon in a record time of 3 hours 47 minutes 39 seconds. Okay, it's not a real snowman, it's actually the UK's David Smith, who ran the Luton Marathon on November 20, 2011.

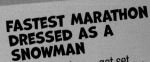

13 MILLION POUNDS OF SNOW

used to build Olympia the snow woman (right). She's only a few feet shorter than the Statue of Liberty!

Eyelashes made from eight pairs of skis

48-ft-wide fleece hat

8-ft-long nose made from chicken wire and painted cheesecloth

Arms made from two 30-ft-tall spruce trees

Lips made from five red car tires

6-ft 6-in-wide snowflake pendant

WOW!

TALLEST SNOWMAN

Residents of the town of Bethel in Maine built a snowman—well, a snow*woman*, technically—measuring 122 ft 1 in (37.21 m) tall. It took the town one month to complete "Olympia" (as she was known), with the finishing touches added on February 26, 2008.

130-ft-long scarf

Three 5-ft-wide truck tires as buttons

SMALLEST MODEL OF A SNOWMAN

This little fellow is nearly two million times smaller than "Olympia," the largest snowman—1,860,500 times smaller, to be precise! He was made by scientists at the UK's National Physical Laboratory—not from snow, but from two microscopic beads of tin. He's so small, he could fit on top of the dot on this letter i.

STAR WARS

THE FORCE IS STRONG IN THIS ONE

WOW!

MOST VIEWED MOVIE TRAILER ON YOUTUBE IN 24 HOURS

The second teaser trailer for *Star Wars: The Force Awakens* was released on YouTube on April 16, 2015. It proved to be a big hit—in just one day, it was viewed 30.65 million times! That works out at just over 21,284 views every minute of the 24-hour period!

$4.05 BILLION

Price paid by Disney to buy Lucasfilm—creators of the *Star Wars* franchise—in October 2012.

LARGEST *STAR WARS* COSTUMING GROUP

The Star Wars 501st Legion (USA) is the world's largest group dedicated to dressing up as *Star Wars* characters. What began as a "stormtrooper fan club" in 1997 is now an 8,122-strong force to be reckoned with in September 2015. The group re-creates the outfits of the movies' bad guys—Imperial troopers, Sith lords, and bounty hunters—but despite this, they're often involved in raising money for good causes!

MOST VIEWED SCI-FI ANIMATION TV SHOW

Star Wars: The Clone Wars was a CGI animated TV series set between *Episode II: Attack of the Clones* and *Episode III: Revenge of the Sith*. It first appeared on the Cartoon Network in 2008, where it had an average viewership of 4 million people in its first two weeks, and an average of 2.3 million across the series.

HIGHEST BOX-OFFICE GROSS BY A SCI-FI SERIES

Star Wars is the most successful science-fiction movie series ever. The first six films collectively grossed $4.4 billion at the worldwide box office, according to figures from The Numbers. Within the series, the **highest-grossing Star Wars movie** is *Episode I: The Phantom Menace*, which has earned $1.007 billion. Will this now be beaten by *Episode VII*?

LARGEST *STAR WARS* SCULPTURE

How cool is this? It's a *Star Wars*-inspired sculpture made from snow that towered 49 ft tall and stretched 75 ft across (15 x 23 m). It looks like it could've been made on the planet Hoth from *The Empire Strikes Back*, but it was actually crafted by soldiers in Hokkaido, Japan, as part of the 66th Sapporo Snow Festival in February 2015.

WHAT ARE YOU WAITING FOR? READ ON!!!!!

STAR WARS

MAY THE FORCE BE WITH YOU

LARGEST LEGO® SCULPTURE BY NUMBER OF BRICKS

A full-size *Star Wars* X-wing fighter was built from 5,335,200 LEGO bricks in Kladno, Czech Republic, in May 2013. The model is based on the LEGO *Star Wars* set #9493, but is 42 times larger—that's why it took 32 builders to construct it!

17,336 HOURS

Time taken to build the full-size X-wing fighter from LEGO bricks (left)—the equivalent of two full years of construction!

MOST VALUABLE *STAR WARS* ACTION FIGURE

An early version of the 1978 Darth Vader action figure typically sells today for $6,000–7,000. Why is it so expensive? Because Vader is the rarest of the figures that came with a "telescopic" lightsaber accessory. The lightsabers broke easily so were soon abandoned.

HIGHEST-RATED *MINECRAFT* ADD-ON BASED ON A MOVIE FRANCHISE

The "Star Wars Classic Skin Pack (Trial)" allows fans of *Minecraft* and *Star Wars* to enjoy both of their favorite franchises at the same time. The character pack contains skins from characters featured in the original *Star Wars* movie trilogy.

WOW!

MOST PROLIFIC VIDEO-GAME SERIES BASED ON A LICENSED PROPERTY

There had been 135 *Star Wars* video games released across 44 different platforms as of 16 July 2015. The first game—named simply *Star Wars*—appeared in arcades in 1983; the latest game in the series, *Battlefront* (pictured), is due for release in November 2015 and is set to be one of the biggest titles of the year.

BIGGEST-SELLING *STAR WARS* VIDEO GAME

Lego Star Wars: The Complete Saga (Traveller's Tales, 2007) is far, far away the biggest-selling game based on the *Star Wars* franchise. As of June 23, 2015, it had sold 14.78 million copies on Nintendo Wii, Nintendo DS, PC, PlayStation 3, and Xbox 360. In the game, you are tasked with collecting gold coins and completing story lines from the first six movies in the series.

CHECK OUT THE AMAZING *STAR WARS* COLLECTOR

AN INTERVIEW WITH: STEVE SANSWEET

Steve took part in this epic photoshoot for Guinness World Records at Rancho Obi-Wan. As we were setting up, he talked about his love for the *Star Wars* saga:

Why are you such a big fan of the movies?
The movies are great fun, the effects still hold up decades later, the characters stand out, and in the battle between good and evil—between the powerful and the seemingly powerless—the good guys win!

Why did you start collecting?
I've always been a collector of something—from baseball cards and bottle caps to comic books. I also developed

a strong love for science fiction and fantasy through reading when I was young, so my two passions merged.

What's the most expensive item?
Probably a Darth Vader costume, parts of which were used in the filming of *Star Wars* and *The Empire Strikes Back*, and as an official "appearance" costume.

LARGEST COLLECTION OF STAR WARS MEMORABILIA

There are few people as passionate about *Star Wars* as Steve Sansweet (USA). His love for the movies has driven him to collect and catalog 93,260 unique items, ranging from official action figures and licensed toys to pinball machines, full-size mannequins, and even props used in the movies. If you're in northern California, you can see the collection for yourself—it's open to the public at Rancho Obi-Wan in Petaluma, Sonoma County.

500,000 ITEMS

are still to be cataloged, says Steve, but it will take him years to complete the count ... and his collection is growing every day as he adds new items!

THE LORD OF THE RINGS

... AND THE HOBBIT!

WOW!

LARGEST BATTLE SEQUENCES ON FILM

The J. R. R. Tolkien movie trilogies—*The Lord of the Rings* and *The Hobbit*—are famous for their epic battle sequences. One of the reasons that these scenes are so spectacular is that they depict more than 200,000 fighting characters. In order to achieve this, the New Zealand special-effects company Weta Digital wrote their own crowd-simulation software called "Massive." This program mixes live-action footage and digital animation with an artificial intelligence that governs how the characters interact.

"Now it is time to show them my true power!"

TOUGHEST ENEMY IN *THE LORD OF THE RINGS ONLINE*

Thorog is a Helegrod Dragon resurrected by Fell spirits in the MMORPG *The Lord of the Rings Online*, published by Turbine (USA). With a total health of 316,961 and power of 52,699, Thorog is the hardest enemy to defeat in the game. If you kill him, you earn the title "De-animator of Thorog."

12.5 MILLION PLASTIC RINGS

were made by the costume team to simulate chain-mail armor for the first *LotR* movie.

FIRST FEATURE FILM SHOT AND PROJECTED AT 48 FRAMES PER SECOND

The Hobbit: An Unexpected Journey (2012) tells the story of the enchanted One Ring and features Gollum (above), who also appears in *The Lord of the Rings.* This was the first major movie to be filmed and projected at 48 frames per second (fps) instead of the regular 24 fps. Filming at such a high speed gives a smoother, sharper image and, in the words of the director, Peter Jackson, results in "a much more lifelike and comfortable viewing experience."

KIRAN SHAH
SHORTEST STUNTMAN

When moviemakers need a stunt double for a short actor—or a Hobbit—they turn to Kiran Shah: the world's **shortest living stuntman** …

"Little Kiran," as he's known, is a 4-ft 1.7-in (126.3-cm) British stunt actor who stood in for Hobbit-size Elijah Wood in the original *LotR* movies. Kiran is a member of the British Equity Stunt Register and has appeared in more than 50 movies, performing stunts in at least 31 of them.

The diminutive daredevil started his stunt career when he doubled for a nine-year-old child in the 1977 movie *Candleshoe.* He was then hired for the 1978 *Superman* movie as a "perspective stunt double"—he was filmed against a small version of the set to make him look as tall as leading man Christopher Reeve!

BEST-SELLING HACK-AND-SLASH VIDEO GAME

"Hack and slash" video games require a lot of … well, hacking and slashing with swords and axes, so it's a genre perfectly suited to Tolkien! The best-selling hack-and-slash of them all is 2002's *The Lord of the Rings: The Two Towers* by Electronic Arts, which had sold 6.65 million copies worldwide as of July 2015.

JURASSIC WORLD

"BIGGER, SCARIER ... MORE TEETH!"

WOW!

FASTEST TIME FOR A MOVIE TO GROSS $1 BILLION

Jurassic World (2015) took just 13 days to earn $1 billion in global ticket sales. This is faster than movies such as *Furious 7* (17 days), *The Avengers*, and *Harry Potter and the Deathly Hallows: Part 2* (both 19 days).

$524 MILLION

This is how much *Jurassic World* earned worldwide in its first weekend on general release—the **highest box-office gross for an opening weekend**.

MOST BANKABLE HOLLYWOOD FIGURE

Steven Spielberg (USA), director of the original *Jurassic Park* (1993), is the most successful person in Hollywood. This is according to The-Numbers.com's "Bankability Index" and is based on the money Spielberg makes and the value he brings to the film industry. As of June 2015, Spielberg's annual value was rated at an impressive $28.4 million. He is pictured here with US producer Kathleen Kennedy, who herself set the record for **highest box-office gross for a movie producer**.

HIGHEST-GROSSING MONSTER MOVIE SERIES

As of July 1, 2015, the *Jurassic Park* franchise had grossed $3.42 billion at the international box office from its four movies: *Jurassic Park* (1993), *The Lost World: Jurassic Park* (1997), *Jurassic Park III* (2001), and *Jurassic World* (2015).

The series is based on the novels *Jurassic Park* and *The Lost World* by the American sci-fi/thriller writer Michael Crichton. Before the first book was even published, director Steven Spielberg paid $1.5 million for the movie rights.

MOST EXPENSIVE TV RIGHTS FOR A MOVIE

America's Fox network paid a record $81 million for the TV rights to *The Lost World: Jurassic Park*. Amazingly, Fox bought the broadcasting rights before the movie was even released on the international market in May 1997.

MORE DINOS THIS WAY!

JURASSIC WORLD

THE REAL STARS OF THE PREHISTORIC WORLD

1,000 DIAMOND-SHAPE TEETH in the mouth of *Edmontosaurus*, the **dinosaur with the most teeth**; it was a herbivore!

FASTEST DINOSAUR

Experts reckon that the speediest dino of all was *Gallimimus*—the ostrichlike creatures that made an appearance in the first *Jurassic Park* movie. This 26-ft-long (8-m) birdlike beast may have been able to run for long periods of time at speeds of 25–35 mph (40–60 km/h)—faster than Usain Bolt at his top speed! The Latin name *Gallimimus* means "chicken mimic" and refers to the dinosaur's roosterlike neck, head, and "beak."

TALLEST DINOSAUR

Sauroposeidon stood 60 ft (18 m) tall—three times taller than a giraffe—and weighed 66 tons (60 metric tonnes), or twice the weight of a fully loaded fire truck. It lived in the mid-Cretaceous period, about 110 million years ago.

LARGEST CARNIVOROUS DINOSAUR

The biggest meat-eating dinosaur, and possibly the largest land-base predator ever known, is *Spinosaurus*. Scientists in Italy calculated that this fearsome beast measured 56 ft (17 m) long and weighed 15,400–19,800 lb (7–9 metric tonnes). This means that *Spinosaurus* was 14 ft (4 m) longer than fellow therapod *Tyrannosaurus rex*. *Spinosaurus* roamed what is now the Sahara desert, 100 million years ago during the Cretaceous period.

LARGEST ARMORED DINOSAUR

Ankylosaurus was a 4.4-ton (4-metric-tonne) herbivore protected with thick plates and a double row of spikes running down from the back of its head to its club tail. Only its belly was left unplated.

LONGEST DINOSAUR HORNS

Triceratops (meaning "three face horns") was a rhinoceros-like dinosaur as big as an SUV. It had a large bony frill around its head, a stubby horn above its nose, and two extra-long horns above the eyes, each measuring 3 ft (1 m). Scientists can't agree on what the frill was for, but they think that the horns were used in jousts with other triceratops.

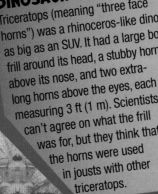

LARGEST PTEROSAUR

With a wingspan of 40–50 ft (12–15 m), the largest pterosaur—and the **largest flying animal** ever—was as wide as two giraffes are tall. Named *Quetzalcoatlus northropi* ("kwet-zal-coat-lus north-rop-eye"), this airborne reptile soared over what is now North America around 70 million years ago. Despite its size, it didn't weigh much because—like a bird—its bones were hollow, helping it to take flight.

BRUCE THE MOSASAUR

Jurassic World introduced movie audiences to *Mosasaurus*—the enormous, carnivorous marine reptile seen leaping from the pool at the open-air "feeding show." But how does the real thing compare?

In the movie, the mosasaur is massive, measuring about 60 ft (18 m) long. In reality, the larger specimens were 40–50 ft (12–15 m). We know this because of Bruce, the **largest mosasaur on display**. Bruce "lives" at the Canadian Fossil Discovery Centre in Manitoba, Canada, and stretches 43 ft (13.1 m) from nose to tail.

Could a creature this big ever leap so high out of the water, like it does in the movie? Probably not. At about 5.5 tons (5 metric tonnes), a 50-ft mosasaur would be too heavy to leave the water, never mind the 15-ton (13.5-metric tonne) beast that features on screen.

STRONGEST BITE FOR A LAND ANIMAL

In February 2012, scientists in the UK built a 3D digital model of a *T. rex* skull. They then added muscles to work out the force with which the dinosaur could snap its jaws shut. The result, measured at the back teeth, was 57,000 Newtons—equivalent to the force of a medium-size elephant sitting on the ground!

All of a *T. rex*'s teeth were shaped like daggers

There were no flat teeth to grind up food; *T. rex* used its sharp teeth to tear off huge chunks of meat and swallow them whole!

"Hinge-and-slip" joint in the jaw allowed *T. rex* to bite things larger than its own head!

THE AVENGERS

WHEN ONE SUPERHERO JUST ISN'T ENOUGH!

$2.89 BILLION
Box-office takings so far from *The Avengers* and *Avengers: Age of Ultron*.

WOW!

MOST VIEWED MOVIE TRAILER (OFFICIAL)

The teaser for Marvel's *Avengers: Age of Ultron* movie had received 77,200,259 views on YouTube by September 16, 2015. According to Digital Spy, it was viewed 26.2 million times on the video-sharing site within the first 24 hours of its upload on October 22, 2014.

HIGHEST ANNUAL EARNINGS FOR A MOVIE ACTOR

Avengers and *Iron Man* star Robert Downey Jr. (USA, left) earned a whopping $80 million in 2014–15, making him Hollywood's highest-earning actor. His salary works out at a superheroic sum of almost $220,000 a day, making him nearly as rich as Tony Stark!

FARTHEST HAMMER THROW

Thor's not the only one breaking things with a hammer … On August 31, 2014, at the Olympic Stadium in Berlin, Germany, Anita Włodarczyk of Poland broke a world record in the sport of hammer throwing. She threw her ball and chain a distance of 261 ft 1 in (79.58 m), smashing the women's world record.

LARGEST YO-YO

Captain America's shield provided the design inspiration for Beth Johnson's titanic toy. It took the Ohio mother three years to build her yo-yo, which is not surprising considering that it's 11 ft 10 in (3.62 m) wide—twice as tall as Beth herself. And at 2.31 tons (2,095.6 kg), you'd need to have the strength of Captain America to play with it!

$1.51 BILLION

Box-office takings from the first *Avengers* movie, making it the **highest-grossing movie based on a comic book.**

DON'T MAKE ME ANGRY. YOU WOULDN'T LIKE ME WHEN I'M ANGRY.

THE AVENGERS

THE HULK ... IN BULK

6 ISSUES
were released of the *Incredible Hulk* comic in 1962–63 before it was canceled. But the Hulk lived on by becoming a founding member of the Avengers a few months later.

1,400 POUNDS
Weight quoted for Savage Hulk in the Marvel Wiki database; in terms of height, he's listed at 8 ft (2.43 m). Being an 8-ft-tall monster is not a requirement for this Hulk mass participation record attempt!

LARGEST GATHERING OF PEOPLE DRESSED AS THE HULK

If there's one color that's most associated with the Irish, it's green. Add to that some purple pants and a black wig and you have all the ingredients for a Hulkathon! At the Muckno Mania Festival held in Castleblayney, Ireland, on July 13, 2012, a total of 574 people got together as their favorite big green guy … and set a new Guinness World Records title in the process.

X-MEN

TAKING SUPERHEROES TO THE X-TREME

$492,937.50
Amount paid for the **most expensive X-Men comic**— a first issue from 1963 of *X-Men* #1. It was sold in 2012 by Heritage Auctions (USA) to an anonymous bidder.

MOST X-MEN CHARACTERS IN A SINGLE VIDEO GAME

The X-Men game featuring the most characters taken from the pages of the Marvel comics is *X-Men Legends II: Rise of Apocalypse*. The PlayStation 2 and Xbox versions of this epic action role-playing game feature 42 official X-Men characters, including 15 playable heroes, four unlockable secret characters, and 23 villains.

LARGEST COLLECTION OF X-MEN MEMORABILIA

As of June 28, 2012, Eric Jaskolka of West Des Moines, Iowa, had collected an incredible 15,400 different items of X-Men memorabilia. Eric started collecting just the comic books back in 1989, then got into the action figures in 1991. Finally, in 1994, he just started collecting anything related to the X-Men franchise!

$3.05 BILLION
Total amount taken at the box office worldwide by the seven X-Men movies. *X-Men: Days of Future Past* was the most lucrative, earning $748.1 million!

MOST MAGNETIC OBJECT IN THE UNIVERSE

The X-Men's archenemy Magneto can manipulate magnetic fields and even generate wormholes. But he's not the most magnetic thing in the universe. That record goes to a type of star known as a magnetar—a star so dense that a piece the size of just your thumb would weigh more than 100 million tons (90.7 million tonnes). It would generate a magnetic field billions of times stronger than any magnet on Earth. If you got to within 1,000 mi (1,600 km) of a magnetar, its magnetic field would turn you—and probably even Magneto—to mush!

WOW!

MOST MOVIES ADAPTED FROM THE WORK OF ONE COMIC-BOOK CREATOR

The creations of Stan Lee (USA) had been adapted into Hollywood films a record 21 times as of March 5, 2015. The franchises are based on comics featuring X-Men, Spider-Man, Daredevil, Hulk, the Fantastic Four, Iron Man, and Captain America. This count rises to 23 if you include Thor—a character that Stan "The Man" reimagined from a Norse myth.

CHALLENGE

LET THE MINION MADNESS COMMENCE!

LARGEST GATHERING OF PEOPLE DRESSED AS MINIONS

If you're a fan of the world's favorite yellow henchmen, this is the perfect record for you. All you have to do is gather together a group from your school or local neighborhood (minimum 250) and stock up on Minion accessories and yellow body paint!

TOP TRIVIA

Minions have three fingers on each hand.

The Minions are largely voiced by the directors of the *Despicable Me* movies, Pierre Coffin (France) and Chris Renaud (USA).

The characters were partly inspired by the Jawas from *Star Wars* and the Oompa-Loompas in *Willy Wonka & The Chocolate Factory*.

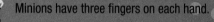

5
HAIRDOS
Number of hairstyles that Minions have in the movies, although one of these is bald!

THE RULES

For the full guidelines and to apply, head to **www.guinnessworldrecords.com/blockbusters**.

1. All participants must be dressed in a complete Minion costume consisting of *at least* the following items:
   a. **Blue long-legged dungarees**
   b. **Goggles (one or two eyes)**
   c. **Black gloves**
   d. **Black footwear**
   e. **Arms, face, neck, and chest must be yellow (use either body paint or clothing)**

2. The costumes must be preapproved by Guinness World Records.

3. All participants must gather in position and remain in a group for at least 5 minutes.

4. A loud start and finish signal must be used. Two experienced timekeepers (e.g. from a local sports club) must time the attempt with stopwatches accurate to 0.01 seconds.

5. The attempt must take place at a single location, such as a gymnasium or a community center.

HOW TO BE A MINION
Here are our top tips for looking despicably dapper. Remember that this is just a guide, but it will give you a good idea of what we're looking for. Some things (such as the hat) are optional, while others (the goggles, for example) are essential to satisfy the rules.

Black gloves (don't worry, five fingers are acceptable!)

Yellow cap/hood is a nice finishing touch but is not obligatory

Goggles are a must! Can be one- or two-eyed

The face must be painted yellow

Yellow torso: wear a long-sleeved T-shirt or hoodie, or use body paint

Dungarees—preferably denim

A Minion "onesie" outfit fulfills a lot of the requirements

Black shoes/boots are the required footwear

DREAMWORKS

HOME TO OGRES, DRAGONS & FIGHTING PANDAS

FIRST MOVIE WITH DIGITAL WATER

The first movie to use computer software to simulate the properties of water was DreamWorks' 1998 animation *Antz*. Before this, fluid effects had to be drawn frame by frame. *Antz* was DreamWorks' first animated feature film. It included multiple scenes involving water, from single drops to a vast flood, to show off that animators could make liquids look realistic.

$175 MILLION

Budget for *Monsters vs Aliens* (2009), the most expensive movie made by DreamWorks Animation, according to The-Numbers.com.

HIGHEST-GROSSING STOP-MOTION ANIMATION

Stop-motion animation involves making a tiny change to a model, taking a snapshot, then making another tiny change. After months, even years, of this, you end up with a movie. The most successful stop-motion movie is *Chicken Run*, by Aardman Animations (UK) in partnership with DreamWorks, which earned $225 million in 2000.

WOW!

MOST SUCCESSFUL ANIMATION STUDIO

DreamWorks Animation SKG—creators of *How to Train Your Dragon* (pictured), *Shrek*, *Kung Fu Panda*, and *Madagascar*—is the most successful animation studio at the box office. Since *Antz* (above left) in 1998, it has grossed a staggering $13.27 billion in movie theaters. Its most successful movie is *Shrek 2* (2004; see right for more Shrek ogreness).

36

SHORTEST DONKEY

Did you know that Shrek's best friend Donkey is based on a real animal? Pericles—or Perry to his friends—is a miniature donkey who lives in Bol Park in Palo Alto, California. Perry is small, but he's not as dinky as the world's smallest donkey. That record is held by KneeHi (above), who's just 25.2 in (64.01 cm) tall and who lives at Best Friends Farm in Gainesville, Florida.

500 PEOPLE

worked on the making of *How to Train Your Dragon 2.* The film grossed $616 million worldwide, which works out at $1.23 million grossed for every person hired!

HIGHEST-GROSSING DAY FOR AN ANIMATION

In just one day—Saturday, May 19, 2007, to be exact—*Shrek the Third* grossed $47 million at the worldwide box office. This is the most money ever made by an animated movie in 24 hours. The hit sequel then went into *ogre*-drive and *swamp*-ed the competition, becoming the most successful animation of that year.

37

STUDIO GHIBLI

TAKING JAPANESE ANIME TO THE BIG SCREEN

2 BATMEN

Many a Hollywood star has lent their voice to the English versions of Ghibli films, including two Batman actors: Michael Keaton in *Porco Rosso* (1992) and Christian Bale in *Howl's Moving Castle* (2004).

HIGHEST-GROSSING JAPANESE ANIME MOVIE

Studio Ghibli's most successful film (see Top 5, right), *Spirited Away* (2001) follows a girl called Chihiro who gets mixed up with witches, demons, and all kinds of weird creatures in an abandoned amusement park that has been converted into a bathhouse. It certainly cleaned up at the box office, taking $274.9 million worldwide, and is also Japan's highest-grossing movie to date.

TOP 5 HIGHEST-GROSSING GHIBLI MOVIES

1. **Spirited Away**
   $274,949,886

2. **Howl's Moving Castle** (right)
   $237,814,327

3. **Ponyo**
   $205,312,666

4. **Princess Mononoke** (below)
   $150,350,000

5. **The Wind Rises**
   $117,924,700

Sources: The Numbers, where data available; (July 2015)

MOST BIOLUMINESCENT BUG

One of the studio's earliest releases was poignant wartime tale *Grave of the Fireflies* (1988), in which a brother and sister—Seita and Setsuko—are forced to rely on their own resources to survive after their house is destroyed. To illuminate their shelter, they capture fireflies, a type of flying beetle that glows to attract a mate by mixing in its abdomen a series of chemicals that emit an eerie light.

MOST SUCCESSFUL FOREIGN-LANGUAGE ANIMATION STUDIO

Since 1997, with the release of *Princess Mononoke*, Studio Ghibli has had a distribution deal with Disney that has seen its profits soar. The 11 subsequent titles—which include the classic *Howl's Moving Castle* (left)—have grossed well over $1 billion. Since 2014, the studio has been on a hiatus from making films.

DID YOU KNOW?

A new species of velvet worm from Vietnam, *Eoperipatus totoros*, which came to light in 2007, was named after *My Neighbor Totoro* (1988) as a result of its resemblance to the Catbus character, a flying cat with caterpillar-like legs.

FASTEST TIME TO MAKE 100 PAPER CRANES

Origami—the art of folding paper—is one of Japan's most well-known traditions and it makes appearances in several Ghibli productions. Folders don't come much faster than Yoneyama Yuichi (Japan), who flew through 100 cranes in just 40 minutes 35 seconds at Nishi Yogo School in Nagoya, Japan, on November 30, 2010. That's an average of 24.35 seconds per bird!

MOVIES
DISNEY
PIRATES OF THE CARIBBEAN ... AND BEYOND

WOW!

HIGHEST-GROSSING PIRATE MOVIE SERIES

The four movies in the *Pirates of the Caribbean* series have hauled in a billion-dollar booty worthy of a swashbuckler such as Jack Sparrow. *The Curse of the Black Pearl* (2003), *Dead Man's Chest* (2006), *At World's End* (2007), and *On Stranger Tides* (2011) earned in a buccaneering box-office take of $3,710,254,215—an average of $927.5 million per movie. Well, shiver me timbers!

$900 MILLION

Estimated cost of making the four *Pirates of the Caribbean* movies. The costliest was *At World's End*—at $300 million, it's the second most expensive movie ever made after *Avatar*!

LARGEST GATHERING OF PIRATES

If you're looking for the pirate capital of the world, you should visit Hastings in East Sussex, on the south coast of the UK. Each year, the town hosts a Pirate Day, in which the locals and visitors dress as swashbucklers. The biggest Pirate Day ever was July 22, 2012, when 14,231 piratical participants descended on Pelham Beach.

MOST SODA CANS OPENED BY A PARROT IN ONE MINUTE

The reason we associate parrots with pirates is because of Robert Louis Stevenson, author of the 1883 novel *Treasure Island*. In the book, the pirate Long John Silver has a parrot—Captain Flint—perched on his shoulder. The pirate's foul-mouthed feathered friend didn't have much use ... unlike Zac the macaw, here. Zac opened 35 drinks cans using just his beak in San Jose, California, on January 12, 2012.

$13.5 MILLION

In 2011, real pirates from Somalia hijacked a tanker containing two billion barrels of oil. They then demanded—and received—this record-breaking ransom: the **highest ransom paid to pirates.**

BEST-SELLING PIRATE-THEMED VIDEO GAME

Yarr, me hearties! There have been many pirate-inspired video games over the years, but *Assassin's Creed IV: Black Flag* (2013, left) has hooked in the most gamers. The sixth main installment in Ubisoft's stealth series, *Black Flag* had sold 12.36 million units as of July 24, 2015, transporting players back to the 18th-century Caribbean.

MOVIES

DISNEY

THE HOUSE OF THE MOUSE

MOST OSCARS WON IN A LIFETIME

Walter "Walt" Elias Disney (USA, 1901–66) won more Academy Awards—aka Oscars—than any other person. He was nominated 64 times (**most Oscar nominations received**) and won 26 of them. He also achieved the record for **most Oscars won consecutively**, winning a statue for eight years in a row (1932–39).

HIGHEST-GROSSING OPENING WEEKEND FOR AN ORIGINAL MOVIE

Most of the blockbuster movies to make it into the record books are sequels and prequels, or based on an existing story—or both! *Inside Out* (2015), however, is a brand new idea from the Disney-owned Pixar Animation Studios. Even though audiences had no prior knowledge of the story, they saw the movie in their droves, and in its first weekend it took a mind-blowing $90.4 million!

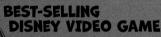

BEST-SELLING DISNEY VIDEO GAME

With 6.4 million copies sold as of March 6, 2015, the original *Kingdom Hearts* (2002) is the biggest-selling video game licensed by the Walt Disney Company. The action role-playing game mashes together Disney characters with those from the *Final Fantasy* game series by Square Enix.

WOW!

MOST VISITED THEME PARK

Magic Kingdom Park at Walt Disney World in Bay Lake, Florida, is the world's most popular theme park. In 2014, at least 19.3 million visitors passed through the park—an average of nearly 53,000 people a day! It's no wonder that Disney describes the Magic Kingdom as "the most magical place on Earth."

MOST EXPENSIVE ANIMATION

Tangled (2010) is Disney's version of the Rapunzel fairy tale. As of September 2015, it's the all-time most expensive animated movie, costing an estimated $260 million. This is the sixth biggest budget of any movie ever made and *Tangled* is also the only animation in the top 20 list of the most expensive films of all time. Much of the budget was spent on developing the technology used to create the computer-generated imagery.

107 ACRES

Area covered by Magic Kingdom Park's six themed "lands"—an area equivalent to more than 82 football fields!

TOP 10

MOVIES

ANIMATED MOVIES

1 FROZEN
$1,274,234,980

This 2013 Disney remake of Hans Christian Andersen's story about an Ice Queen was always going to be big, but no one could predict it would be THIS big! The tale about royal sisters Elsa and Anna quickly shot to the top of the all-time animation chart. A spin-off short called *Frozen Fever* hit movie theaters, alongside *Cinderella*, in March 2015, but fans will have to wait until 2018 for the full-feature sequel, *Frozen 2*.

2 TOY STORY 3
$1,069,818,229

The third installment of the toys-to-life tale sees favorites Buzz, Woody, Jessie, and co. planning a great escape from day care, where they're terrorized by tearaway tots intent on destruction! The most successful movie in the series, it earned a much-deserved Best Picture nomination at the 2011 Oscars.

3 THE LION KING
$987,480,140

We have Shakespeare to thank for the third movie in our list: the story of Simba and his journey to reclaim his rightful title of king of the jungle is actually based on the Bard's play *Hamlet*. Throw in some African mythology—and music by Elton John and Tim Rice—and you have all the ingredients for a truly blockbusting phenomenon.

4 DESPICABLE ME 2
$974,758,842

It might have been beaten by *Frozen* at the Oscars (losing out on both Best Animated Movie and Best New Song), but this despicable sequel remains Universal Studio's most profitable movie. Gru and his tiny yellow henchmen are already signed up for a three-quel in 2017.

5 FINDING NEMO
$936,429,370

The fishy tale follows clownfish Marlin on his adventure from the Great Barrier Reef—at 1,260 mi (2,027 km), the **longest reef**—in search of missing son Nemo. A sequel centered on forgetful fish Dory (blue tang above), voiced by TV star Ellen DeGeneres, is slated for release in 2016.

6 SHREK 2
$932,252,921

Forget fearsome fire-breathing dragons and the evil Lord Farquaad … Shrek faces his greatest challenge yet: the in-laws! More gags, more songs, and more mayhem, this sequel went on to become the most successful movie of 2004. It also spawned a spin-off movie starring a new character, Puss in Boots (pictured above).

7 ICE AGE: CONTINENTAL DRIFT
$879,765,137

Another sequel, this 2012 hit is the fourth in the Ice Age series. It reunites Manny, Diego, and Sid, and pits them against the piratical Captain Gutt (based on the prehistoric orangutan-like *Gigantopithecus blacki*, which happens to be the world's **largest ever primate**!)

8 MADAGASCAR 3
$746,921,271

Alex, Marty, Gloria, and Melman find themselves roped into a traveling circus as it crosses Europe, providing them with the perfect cover for their attempted trip back home to New York. Along the way, they make new friends and turn the failing circus into a roaring success. Talking of which, this 2012 three-quel turned out to be the biggest hit in the *Madagascar* series.

9 MONSTERS UNIVERSITY
$743,588,329

Pixar's first—and only—prequel takes us back to the college days of pro scarers Michael "Mike" Wazowski and James P. "Sulley" Sullivan and explains how they got their job at the famous Monsters, Inc. company. The movie was frightfully successful, becoming the **highest-grossing college comedy movie**.

10 UP
$731,542,621

One of just four original animations in the top 10—i.e., not a sequel or based on an existing story—the moving *Up* delighted audiences with its grumpy-but-lovable lead character Carl, annoying Wilderness Explorer Russell and talking dog Dug. It also gave Pixar their first Oscar nomination for Best Picture.

TOP 10
LIVE-ACTION MOVIES

1 AVATAR
$2,783,918,982

James Cameron's sci-fi epic is set in the 22nd century and tells the story of the 10-ft-tall (3-m) blue-skinned Na'vi as they battle for survival on the planet Pandora. At least four years in the making, the 2009 movie pioneered numerous film-making techniques—particularly full-performance motion-capture, and 3D computer-generated imagery—and was a blockbusting hit with audiences.

2 TITANIC
$2,207,615,668

Despite the fact that we all knew how it would end—spoiler alert: *Titanic* sinks!—the 1997 story of the demise of the "unsinkable" ship captivated audiences and became the **first movie to gross $1 billion**. It was another megahit for James Cameron, the director of **most movies to gross $1 billion at the worldwide box office** (2).

3 JURASSIC WORLD
$1,565,122,588

Proving that it *is* possible to resurrect old dinosaurs, writer/director Colin Trevorrow breathed new life into Michael Crichton's Jurassic giants in 2015. *Jurassic World* certainly survived the crunch, becoming not only the **fastest movie to gross $100 million** (in 2 days), but also **$500 million** (in 17 days).

4 THE AVENGERS
$1,519,479,547

The Marvel-ous superheroes took movie theaters by storm on their first outing in 2012. The live-actioner, directed by Joss Whedon, became the most successful movie of the year at the box office, and the first Marvel license to earn more than $1 billion worldwide.

5 FURIOUS 7
$1,513,906,673

The tragic and untimely death of actor Paul Walker—in a car crash, ironically—undoubtedly drove fans into theaters to see his final film, which became a memorial to the young star. The seventh movie in the *Fast and the Furious* franchise follows professional street racers as they attempt to carve out a normal life after years as mercenaries; as with real life, not all goes to plan …

6 AVENGERS: AGE OF ULTRON
$1,398,442,728

The Avengers—and director Josh Whedon—make their second appearance in the Top 10 with this 2015 sequel. According to Whedon, his influences for the script were *Star Wars Episode V: The Empire Strikes Back*, *The Godfather Part II*, and *Frankenstein*. It sounds like an odd mix, but it clearly worked!

7 HARRY POTTER AND THE DEATHLY HALLOWS: PART 2
$1,341,511,219

Yet another sequel—the final installment in the Harry Potter saga—and yet another billion-dollar blockbuster. The movie earned $91 million in a single day in the USA alone, earning the record for the **highest-grossing single day at the domestic box office**.

8 IRON MAN 3
$1,215,392,272

This is the third time that Tony Stark—aka Avenger Iron Man—makes an appearance in the Top 10. This time, he's headlining in his own threequel from 2013, battling the supervillain Mandarin—aka mad scientist Aldrich Killian. Robert Downey Jr., who first played Tony Stark in 2008's *Iron Man*, has the role to thank for making him the **highest-paid actor** (and the eighth highest-paid celebrity) in the world.

9 THE LORD OF THE RINGS: THE RETURN OF THE KING
$1,141,408,667

It has the **longest title for a film to win a Best Picture Oscar** (36 characters), and is one of only three movies to win 11 Oscars (**most Oscars won by a movie**). No surprise, then, that the final film in Peter Jackson's *LotR* trilogy—*and the most successful movie of 2003—makes it into the Top 10.

10 TRANSFORMERS: DARK OF THE MOON
$1,123,790,543

The third in the Transformers series, *Dark of the Moon* is set three years after *Revenge of the Fallen*. In the movie, NASA's Apollo Moon-landing program is revealed to have been a ruse to investigate a crashed spacecraft. Could this mysterious vessel help end the war between the Autobots and Decepticons? In a nutshell, yes …

COMICS & BOOKS

COOL COMICS

A PICTURE SAYS A THOUSAND WORDS ...

ACTUAL SIZE

LONGEST-RUNNING WEEKLY COMIC

Dennis the Menace and Gnasher have been wreaking havoc since July 30, 1938. Published by D. C. Thomson, British comic *The Beano* has only stopped printing once, owing to paper shortages in World War II. Two days before its 77th birthday, *The Beano* was on issue #3,794, making it the longest-running weekly comic-book series to have kept both its name and numbering system since its launch.

SMALLEST COMIC BOOK

Drawn and written by Martin Lodewijk (Netherlands), the 16-page-long *Agent 327* was published in 1999 and measured just 1 x 1.4 in (2.5 x 3.7 cm). The publication was so small that everyone who bought one of these tiny comics also received a free magnifying glass! For the opposite end of the spectrum, see the monster on the opposite page!

MOST SYNDICATED COMIC STRIP

Considering that this lasagne-loving cat, created by Indiana-born cartoonist Jim Davis, is well known for being lazy, he sure does get around. In fact, the comic strip, which first debuted in 41 publications in 1978, now appears in around 2,100 newspapers and is estimated to be read by some 200 million people. Over the years, Garfield has starred in TV series, movies, and book compilations in multiple languages (above).

LARGEST COMICS FESTIVAL

Japan is the **greatest comic-reading nation**, with comics, or "manga" as they are known, making up 40% of all printed material sold in the country. It's little wonder, then, that the highest-attended festival—Comiket—also takes place there, in Tokyo. At the 2013 three-day event, some 590,000 visitors attended, and more than 8.7 million publications were sold.

105

Copies printed in the first run of the supersize *CruZader™: Agent of the Vatican*. The giant comic book was priced at $200 in the USA and $300 on the international market.

LARGEST COMIC BOOK

The first chapter of a special scaled-up edition of Kickstarter-funded graphic novel *CruZader™: Agent of the Vatican*, by Omar Morales (USA), was printed as a colossal 28-page comic in 2014. Its cover measured in at 2 ft x 3 ft 1.1 in (60.9 x 94.4 cm).

GOT A LOT OF COMICS? NOT AS MANY AS BOB BRETALL ...

COMICS & BOOKS
COLLECTOR'S CORNER
COMICS

AN INTERVIEW WITH:
BOB BRETALL

Take a leaf out of Bob's book and find out what it's like to be a comic-collecting aficionado:

What made you start collecting?
My older brother gave me a "coupon" good for 10 comics when I was eight. The first comic I bought was *Amazing Spider-Man* #88 and I fell in love with the character, the art (by John Romita Sr.), and the story (by Stan Lee).

What is the last comic that you read?
I read over 100 new comic books every month, so this answer will be different every time you ask it. I'm writing this on July 22, 2015, and the last comic I read was *Starve* #2 (Image Comics).

Any favorite superheroes?
My favorite superhero would have to be Spider-Man, since he got me into collecting. I've always liked the human problems Peter Parker faced.

That said, I would like to emphasize that there are a *lot* of things besides superhero comics out there.

100+ COMICS

Average number of comic books bought by Bob each month. He's also an avid collector of action figures, busts and statues, DVDs, plus James Bond and *Lord of the Rings* memorabilia.

LARGEST COLLECTION OF COMIC BOOKS

As far as comic-book collectors go, computer scientist Bob Bretall from Mission Viejo, California, truly KAPOW-ed the competition to take home this record. As of August 6, 2015, he owned 101,822 unique comics—a figure that continues to rise as he adds new editions and back copies. More amazing still? Bob says that he has read 95% of them!

CHALLENGE

THIS RECORD'S NO PUSHOVER ...

10,489
The **most dominoes toppled underwater by a team**; achieved by multi-domino record holders Sinners Domino Entertainment (Germany) in 2014.

MOST BOOKS TOPPLED IN A DOMINO FASHION IN ONE HOUR

Domino toppling is a classic Guinness World Records activity, and over time it has extended far beyond dominoes (see Top Topplers, below). In this challenge, books take the place of the traditional tiles. Getting your school or local library involved might be a good idea, because you'll need a large room and, of course, a *lot* of books! There's no limit to the number of people who can get involved, but you are against the clock; all the books have to be in position within 60 minutes.

TOP TOPPLERS

DISC CASES

Plates	15,396	Procter & Gamble (Australia)
Coins	12,349	Shinsei Bank, Ltd. (Japan)
Disc cases	5,969	Tim Weissker (Germany)
Humans on mattresses	1,150	Höffner Möbelgesellschaft GmbH. (Germany)
Humans on airbeds (lilos)	553	Johnson & Johnson (Middle East)

HUMANS ON MATTRESSES

MOST BOOKS TOPPLED IN A DOMINO FASHION

For the challenge shown on these pages, you have just one hour to set up the books, but another GWR category has no time limit at all—making for book dominoes on a truly epic scale. On July 2, 2015, Atle Goutbeek (Norway) knocked over 6,535 books, but just 10 days later, Goutbeek, too, was toppled when a dedicated Japanese group, called Longest Book Domino Chain Gifu World Record Challenge 2015, raised the bar to 9,862 books (above). They were seeking to surpass the 10,000 milestone, but nearly 300 books had to be discounted.

THE RULES

For the full guidelines and to apply, head to **www.guinnessworldrecords.com/blockbusters**.

1. All books used in the domino line must be commercially available. Homemade books are not acceptable in this category.

2. Participants have exactly one hour to set up the books. Within that period, the books can be arranged in any way or repositioned if they fall.

3. There is no limit to the number of people who can help set up the books, but the pushover must be done from one point and by *one* person. After the initial book has been toppled, no other book in the assemblage can be touched.

4. A count of standing books must be taken by two independent witnesses during the setup, and then recounted after toppling has occurred. Only books that fall down count toward the final total. Both counting processes must be filmed.

SUPERMAN

IS IT A BIRD? IS IT A PLANE? NO, IT'S ...

FIRST SUPERHERO ON TELEVISION

It probably comes as no surprise that Superman—the first genuine superhero (see opposite page)—was also the first to make it on to the small screen. *Adventures of Superman* debuted in 1952, in black and white, and was sponsored by the cereal company Kellogg's. It starred George Reeves as Clark Kent/ Superman (pictured), whose distinctive red and blue figure-hugging costume wouldn't be seen in color until the series went into syndication in 1965.

867 SUPER-MEN, -WOMEN, AND -CHILDREN AT KENDAL CALLING

LARGEST GATHERING OF PEOPLE DRESSED AS SUPERMAN

Back in 2008, the city of Metropolis—yes, the *real* Metropolis—in Illinois set a new record for gathering together 122 people dressed as Superman. The record has changed hands many times since and is now held by the fancy-dress store Escapade of London, UK—on July 27, 2013, they dressed 867 participants at the Kendal Calling music festival in Lowther Deer Park, Cumbria, UK.

SUPERMAN
VIDEO COMPUTER SYSTEM
GAME PROGRAM
ONE PLAYER

SPECIAL EDITION

CX 2631

FIRST COMIC-BOOK SUPERHERO TO FEATURE IN A VIDEO GAME

The DC Comics superstar got the video-game treatment in 1979 with the release of *Superman* on the Atari 2600. Controlling the 8-bit Superman, you were tasked with rebuilding Metropolis Memorial Bridge after its destruction by Lex Luthor, then capturing the crime boss and his gang members.

$130

The paltry sum that the creators of Superman earned when they sold the rights to their comic book hero. Today, the Superman brand is worth more than $1 billion!

WOW!

FIRST SUPERHERO WITH SUPERPOWERS

Superman made his comics debut— in *Action Comics* #1 (April 18, 1938)— with out-of-this-world abilities never before seen in comic books. In the first issue, he was invulnerable to knives, ran faster than an express train, and leaped tall buildings in a single bound. In later issues, he demonstrated heightened senses, such as X-ray vision, superstrength, and the ability to fly. Below is a display of his solar-beam eyes in the 1978 *Superman* movie starring Christopher Reeve.

MOST EXPENSIVE COMIC

The table on the right shows the most valuable comic books currently sought by collectors and dealers. This is what comic experts Nostomania believe people will pay today for an edition in the very best condition. The most *actually* paid for a comic ever was $3,207,852 for *Action Comics* #1. It was bought by Metropolis Collectibles (USA) during an eBay auction on August 24, 2014.

TOP 5 MOST VALUABLE COMICS

Collectors will pay a *lot* of money for old comic books. Here are the five editions valued more highly than any others:

1. Action Comics #1
$5,300,000

2. Detective Comics #27
$2,850,000

3. Superman #1
$878,000

4. Marvel Comics #1
$751,000

5. Batman #1
$708,000

Source: Nostomania (August 2015)

SPIDER-MAN

IS YOUR SPIDEY SENSE TINGLING?

MOST EXPENSIVE SILVER AGE COMIC

Following the Golden Age of comics (1930s–50s), the Silver Age lasted from 1956 to ca. 1970. The most money anyone has paid for a comic from that era is $1.1 million, for a copy of 1962's *Amazing Fantasy* #15. It was in this issue that Spider-Man first swung into action.

MOST EXPENSIVE THEATER PRODUCTION

With 2011 musical *Spider-Man: Turn Off the Dark*, the web-slinging superhero even left his mark on Broadway and beyond. With production costs running to a whopping $75 million, the budget for the Spidey spectacle set a stage-play record worldwide. The show is due to tour the States in 2015/16.

DID YOU KNOW?

As well as comic books, TV cartoons, and movies, Spider-Man has also been the title star of 36 video games. The first Spider-Man game was released in 1982 for the Atari 2600; the most recent console game was 2014's *The Amazing Spider-Man 2* (left).

MOST BUILDINGS CLIMBED UNASSISTED

Known as "Spider-Man"—despite having vertigo!—urban climber Alain Robert from France scaled 121 towers, skyscrapers, and monuments between 1994 and 2015. Above, he takes on the 600-ft (183-m) Framatome Tower (aka Tour Areva) in Paris, France, in 1998.

HIGHEST-GROSSING MOVIE REBOOT

There have been a lot of familiar faces hitting the big screen in recent years—especially in the superhero genre, with the Hulk, Superman, and Batman all getting fresh new looks. But no movie reboot has been more successful than 2012's *The Amazing Spider-Man*, which took $757,890,267. Just behind it is ape-takeover epic *Dawn of the Planet of the Apes* (2014) on $703,545,589.

2

Number of people bitten by the radioactive spider that gave Peter Parker his powers. The second was Cindy Moon, who developed the same powers and would later go by the name "Silk." Cindy's debut came in the *Amazing Spider-Man* comic-book series in 2014.

MOST PEOPLE DRESSED AS SPIDER-MAN

All kitted out in the classic red-and-blue *Amazing Spider-Man* suit, 438 people swung in to claim this record on July 28, 2015, surpassing the previous mark by 40 Spidey folk. Organized by Australian recruitment company Charterhouse, the event sought to raise funds for children's health charity Life Education, turning the wannabes into real superheroes that day.

WOW!

BATMAN

HOLY BATMANIA! IT'S THE CAPED CRUSADER!

MOST ADAPTED COMIC-BOOK CHARACTER

Batman has starred in eight full-length live-action movies, starting with *Batman* (1966), a feature film version of the popular TV series. His ninth incarnation will pit him against the Man of Steel in *Batman v Superman: Dawn of Justice* (2016, pictured above).

LARGEST COLLECTION OF BATMAN MEMORABILIA

Kevin Silva of Indianapolis, Indiana, has been collecting Batman gear for more than 45 years and now owns 2,501 unique items. His first piece was a Batman lunch box, and his favorite—and probably his most expensive—is an outfit modeled on that worn by Adam West in the 1960s *Batman* TV series (pictured).

MOST EXPENSIVE BATMAN MEMORABILIA SOLD AT AUCTION

Talking of the 1960s TV show, a Batmobile used in the series sold at the Barrett-Jackson car auction in Scottsdale, Arizona, on January 19, 2013, for $4.62 million.

BEST-SELLING VIDEO GAME BASED ON A COMIC BOOK

According to VGChartz, Rocksteady's *Batman: Arkham City* (2011) had sold 10.76 million copies as of September 19, 2015. Arkham—an asylum for Gotham's criminally insane—was introduced into the comic books in *Batman* #258 (October 1974), written by Dennis O'Neil and drawn by Irv Novick. Pictured is the latest Arkham game, 2015's *Batman: Arkham Knight*.

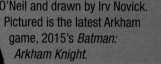

1943
The year in which the Batcave was introduced; until then, the Caped Crusader stored his Batmobile and Batmicrolite in a barn connected to Wayne Manor by an underground tunnel.

CHUCK DIXON
GRAHAM NOLAN
SCOTT HANNA

WOW!

LARGEST AUCTION OF COMIC BOOKS
On May 5 and 6, 2011, Heritage Auction Galleries in New York City raised an incredible $6,077,355 from the sale of comic books, comic art, and comic-related memorabilia.

Among the lots was this original art from issue #3 of *Batman: The Dark Knight Returns* (1986), which sold for $448,125—the single most expensive piece of American comic art to sell at auction.

Picture courtesy of Heritage Auctions, www.ha.com

LONGEST-RUNNING MONTHLY COMIC
Detective Comics, which introduced us to Batman in issue #27 (May 1939), has been printed continuously by DC Comics since issue #1 in March 1937. It's published in two volumes (1937–2011 and 2011–present), and as of February 2015, a total of 927 regular issues had been published across both.

HARRY POTTER

YOU CANNOT BE SIRIUS ...

$2,400
Amount paid in advance to J. K. Rowling by Bloomsbury Publishing for *Harry Potter and The Philosopher's Stone* (1997).

$40,000
Value in 2013 of a Bloomsbury first-edition copy of the book.

HIGHEST-GROSSING FANTASY FILM SERIES

The eight movies in the *Harry Potter* series, released between 2001 and 2011, grossed a total of $6,847,194,908 at the worldwide box office. The most successful entry in the franchise was the last movie, *Harry Potter and the Deathly Hallows: Part 2*, which conjured up a gross of $1,341,511,219 globally.

FASTEST-SELLING CHILDREN'S BOOK

Harry Potter and the Deathly Hallows sold 8.3 million copies in the first 24 hours of being on sale in the USA on July 21, 2007. Fans lined up around the block to be among the first to buy it. Starting at one minute past midnight, the seventh— and final—novel in the *Harry Potter* series sold an average of 345,833 books per hour!

LARGEST MODEL OF HOGWARTS

This model of Hogwarts Castle is a 1:24-scale replica that measures 50 ft (15.24 m) across. It was created by Stuart Craig (pictured) and other members of the Warner Bros. Art Department in 2011, and contains more than 2,500 fiber-optic lights.

450 MILLION

Harry Potter books estimated to be in print—150 million of which sold in the USA. The series still features in the *New York Times'* Best Sellers children's top 10 after 333 weeks, as of August 2015 (see pp. 74–75).

WOW!

FIRST BILLION-DOLLAR AUTHOR

J. K. Rowling (UK), creator of Harry Potter, is one of only five self-made female billionaires. She is also the first billion-dollar author according to the money experts at *Forbes* magazine, who included her as a billionaire for the first time in their 2004 rich list. The seven *Harry Potter* books have sold millions of copies around the world and have been published in at least 55 languages.

LARGEST GATHERING OF PEOPLE DRESSED AS HARRY POTTER

It may not be enchanted, or built on a lake, but Tanbridge House School in Horsham, West Sussex, UK, looks like the closest thing to Hogwarts that a muggle will ever find. On March 5, 2015, a total of 521 pupils dressed up as Harry Potter, complete with Hogwarts uniform, spectacles, a (fake!) forehead scar, a pointed magician's hat, and a magic wand.

MORE WIZARDS AND WITCHCRAFT OVER THE PAGE!

HARRY POTTER

AN INTERVIEW WITH: MENAHEM POTTER

It takes more than magic to be as dedicated a collector as Menahem …

What drew you to Harry Potter colletables?
I was looking for something to inspire my life and fill my longing for illusions. I used to meet with friends in a coffee shop, and one evening nobody was there, so I read through the entire first book without any breaks. I was so amazed that my dream began to enter this magical world through objects.

If you were to ask J. K. Rowling one question, what would it be?
I've been studying English just to talk to her! The first thing I would say is thank you and the first question I would ask is: Would you invite me for a cup of tea?

Any favorite items?
The most valuable object to me is a wall plaque with an image of the Chamber of Secrets. It was made by my mother using recycled materials and was a commemorative gift I received from her one Children's Day.

$24 BILLION

Estimated value of the Harry Potter brand—i.e., books, movies, DVDs, and toys—according to the Statistic Brain Research Institute.

LARGEST COLLECTION OF HARRY POTTER MEMORABILIA

There are few Harry Potter fans as committed to the boy wizard as Menahem Asher Silva Vargas of Mexico City, Mexico. At the last count, on November 5, 2013, Menahem Potter—as he's known to his friends—had 3,097 unique items of Potter paraphernalia.

Among his prized possessions are bedclothes, books, pin badges, caps, and wands.

FEAR FACTOR

PUTTING THE "BOO!" INTO BOOKS

3

Number of Nickelodeon "Favorite Book" awards won by the *Goosebumps* series. Following *Deep Trouble* (1995), *Tales to Give You Goosebumps* took it in 1996, and sequel *Deep Trouble II* won in 1998.

WOW!

MOST PROLIFIC CHILDREN'S HORROR BOOK SERIES

No other books have given kids more heebie-jeebies than *Goosebumps*, with 62 original titles. The first—*Welcome to Dead House*—was published in 1992 and there have since been spin-off series, TV adaptations, and even a 2015 movie (main picture). In 1995, *Deep Trouble* became the first winner of "Favorite Book" at Nickelodeon's Kids' Choice Awards.

MOST PROLIFIC AUTHOR OF KIDS' HORROR FICTION

R. L. Stine (USA) is the undisputed king of children's horror, penning all 62 original *Goosebumps* books, plus other popular series, such as *Fear Street* and *Mostly Ghostly*. In total, his portfolio stands at 300-plus horror books—all of which, in his words, are intended to "give kids the creeps."

MOST PORTRAYED LITERARY CHARACTER IN THE MOVIES

Stake and garlic ready? They should be if you're heading to Hollywood, as no other book character has starred in more movies and TV movies than fang-tastic bloodsucker Dracula: 538 to date! The original "bat-man" has taken many guises, from Bela Lugosi's classic portrayal in 1931 (right) to the owner of a monster vacation resort in *Hotel Transylvania 2* (2015, left).

HIGHEST-GROSSING VAMPIRE MOVIE

Vampires and werewolves got a 21st-century makeover in Stephenie Meyer's top-selling *Twilight* series. The final book—*Breaking Dawn* (2008)—shifted 1.3 million copies on launch day alone. The five tie-in movies, starring Robert Pattinson (UK), Kristen Stewart, and Taylor Lautner (both USA; left to right), have also taken a big bite of the box office; finale *Breaking Dawn: Part 2* (2012) earned $832 million worldwide.

DIARY OF A WIMPY KID

TRIALS AND TRIBULATIONS OF GROWING UP

HIGHEST-GROSSING MOVIE SERIES BASED ON A FICTIONAL CHILDREN'S DIARY

As well as flying off the shelves at bookstores, the fictional diaries of the downtrodden Greg Heffley have also found success at the movies, with three films released to date. *Diary of a Wimpy Kid* (2010, pictured), *Rodrick Rules* (2011), and *Dog Days* (2012) have collectively earned $227,879,203 at the box office, according to The Numbers.

LONGEST KEPT DIARY

Anyone who has ever written a diary will know that sometimes it can be hard to put your thoughts to paper. Colonel Ernest Loftus of Zimbabwe, however, seems to have had no problem. Starting his journal on May 4, 1896, at the age of 12, he updated it daily for a staggering 91 years, until his death in 1987.

MOST EXPENSIVE DIARY AT AUCTION

A diary kept by Dr. Alexander Macklin (UK, above right), which logged the events of Ernest Shackleton's 1914–17 attempt to cross the Antarctic on the *Endurance* Expedition, fetched $153,573 at Christie's in London, UK, in 2001.

The **most expensive *fake* diaries**, meanwhile, were a series of journals, allegedly penned by Adolf Hitler, for which almost $5 million was paid by Germany's *Stern* magazine in 1983. They were later found to be forgeries.

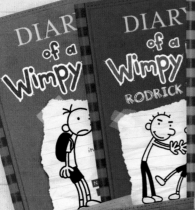

DIARY of a Wimpy Kid

DIARY of a Wimpy RODRICK

DIARY of a Wimpy k THE LAST ST

DIARY of a Wimpy DOG DA

DIARY of a Wimpy Kid THE UGLY TRUTH

DIARY of a Wimpy CABIN F

DIARY of a Wimpy THE THIRD

DIARY of a Wimpy k HARD L

DIARY of a Wimpy THE LONG

DIARY of a Wimpy Kid OLD SCHOOL

WOW!

MOST PRINTED FICTIONAL DIARY SERIES

Since the first title was published in 2007 to the release of the ninth book, *The Long Haul*, in 2014, the *Diary of a Wimpy Kid* series has seen in excess of 150 million copies printed. This is set for another huge boost in November 2015 with the release of *Old School* (above), the 10th installment.

MOST NICKELODEON KIDS' CHOICE AWARDS WON BY A MALE AUTHOR

As if *Wimpy Kid* author Jeff Kinney (USA) needed any further confirmation of his creation's popularity, the series has been voted kids' "Favorite Book" five times. This is just behind *Harry Potter* writer J. K. Rowling (UK) on six—the **most Kids' Choice Awards won by an author**.

335 WEEKS

Time that the *Diary of a Wimpy Kid* series had been on the *New York Times*' best-selling children's series list, as of August 8, 2015—just ahead of *Harry Potter* on 333 weeks.

THE HUNGER GAMES

THE TRILOGY WITH THE ODDS IN ITS FAVOR

WOW!

HIGHEST-GROSSING FEMALE ACTION STAR

The three *Hunger Games* films to date, starring Jennifer Lawrence (USA) as Katniss Everdeen, have been huge hits. Along with two *X-Men* appearances as Raven/ Mystique, Lawrence's action-movie portfolio has grossed $3.3 billion. That girl's on fire!

BEST-SELLING CHILDREN'S SERIES IN A YEAR

While longer-running series, such as *Diary of a Wimpy Kid* (see p. 68), may have sold more copies overall, the *Hunger Games* trilogy shifted an incredible 27.7 million books (counting both physical and digital sales) in 2012–13 alone. This surpassed the previous one-year series best-seller, *Harry Potter*, by 7.9 million copies.

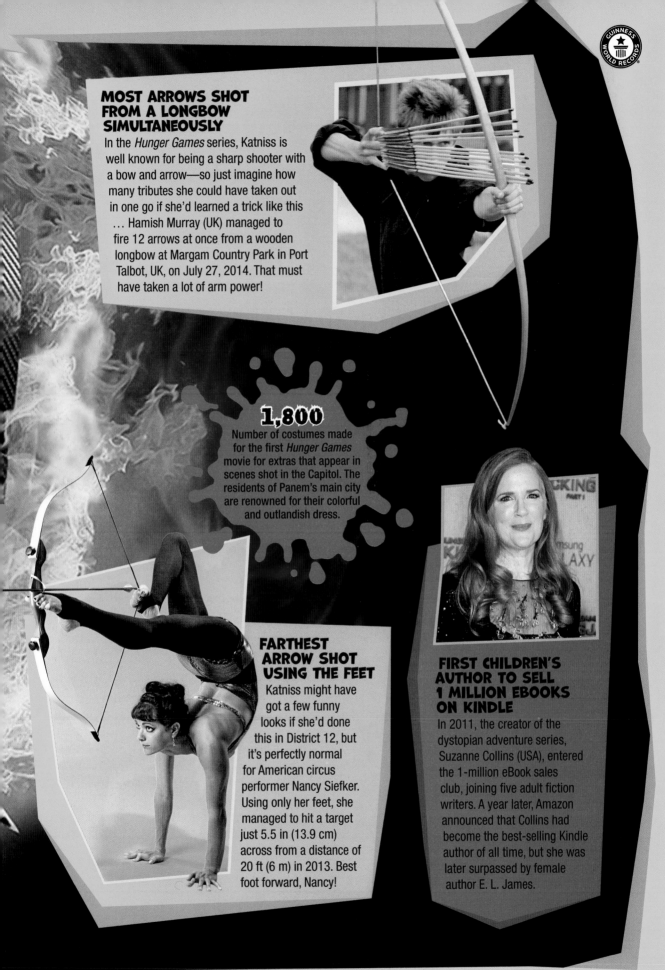

MOST ARROWS SHOT FROM A LONGBOW SIMULTANEOUSLY

In the *Hunger Games* series, Katniss is well known for being a sharp shooter with a bow and arrow—so just imagine how many tributes she could have taken out in one go if she'd learned a trick like this ... Hamish Murray (UK) managed to fire 12 arrows at once from a wooden longbow at Margam Country Park in Port Talbot, UK, on July 27, 2014. That must have taken a lot of arm power!

1,800

Number of costumes made for the first *Hunger Games* movie for extras that appear in scenes shot in the Capitol. The residents of Panem's main city are renowned for their colorful and outlandish dress.

FARTHEST ARROW SHOT USING THE FEET

Katniss might have got a few funny looks if she'd done this in District 12, but it's perfectly normal for American circus performer Nancy Siefker. Using only her feet, she managed to hit a target just 5.5 in (13.9 cm) across from a distance of 20 ft (6 m) in 2013. Best foot forward, Nancy!

FIRST CHILDREN'S AUTHOR TO SELL 1 MILLION EBOOKS ON KINDLE

In 2011, the creator of the dystopian adventure series, Suzanne Collins (USA), entered the 1-million eBook sales club, joining five adult fiction writers. A year later, Amazon announced that Collins had become the best-selling Kindle author of all time, but she was later surpassed by female author E. L. James.

COLLECTOR'S CORNER

GUINNESS WORLD RECORDS

LARGEST COLLECTION OF GUINNESS WORLD RECORDS MEMORABILIA

Britain's Martyn Tovey has made it into the *Guinness World Records* book ... for collecting *Guinness World Records* books! He actually holds two records. The first is for amassing 2,164 items of GWR memorabilia, such as posters, board games, and toys. The second is for his extensive library of 353 *Guinness World Records* books, ranging from the first edition (1955) to the most recent (both above)—the **largest collection of *Guinness World Records* annuals**!

"The books contain more than achievements," says Martyn. "They represent a fascinating record of our recent past."

Aww, shucks—thanks, Martyn!

EDITOR'S CHOICE

Here, GWR Editor-in-Chief Craig Glenday selects some of the most amazing content that you'll find in the world's **best-selling annual books**.

TALLEST RIDABLE MOTORCYCLE

"Nearly 17 ft tall and 33 ft long, this mega motorcycle is six times bigger than the original … and ridable!"

LONGEST TONGUE ON A DOG

"Relatively, if your tongue was as long as Puggy the Pekingese's, you could lick your knees without bending over! It sticks out a whopping 4.5 in!"

LONGEST FINGERNAILS

"At their peak length, the fingernails of Lee Redmond of Salt Lake City, Utah, reached a total of 28 ft 4 in – as long as a school bus!"

MOST HOT DOGS EATEN IN THREE MINUTES

"Takeru Kobayashi of Japan chomped through six whole hot dogs—buns and all!—in three minutes. He also ate 50 dogs in 12 minutes back in 2001. Wow!"

TALLEST MAN

"The last time I measured Turkey's Sultan Kösen, he was a whopping 8 ft 3 in! He's only the 13th person in history over 8 ft tall."

The spellbinding *Harry Potter* books worked their magic to become the **all-time best-selling kids' series** (see pp. 62–65), but with new titles hitting the shelves all the time, best-seller lists change every week in the world of books. Here's a glimpse of some of the most popular series of 2015, based on *The New York Times'* Best Sellers list.

1 THE MAZE RUNNER

This *runner-way* success by US author James Dashner may not be the **best-selling kids' series ever** (see no. 2), but as we went to press it was the best-selling current kids' book series. The post-apocalyptic trilogy centers on Thomas, a teen who wakes up with no memories in a labyrinth that has moving walls and is terrorized by deadly creatures called "Grievers."

Although debuting back in 2009, the series has seen a revival with the release of two action-packed feature movies: *The Maze Runner* in 2014 (inset), which grossed $345,527,862 worldwide, and *The Scorch Trials* in 2015.

Dashner has also penned a prequel to the series, *The Kill Order*, with a follow-up, *The Fever Code*, slated for 2016.

BOOK 1 IN THE *NEW YORK TIMES* BESTSELLING SERIES BY JAMES DASHNER

THE MAZE RUNNER

SOON TO BE A MAJOR MOTION PICTURE

Top 10 based on both print and eBook sales from *The New York Times'* Best Sellers for Children's Series, drawn from the week ending August 8, 2015.

2 HARRY POTTER

Considering that this is the **best-selling children's book series ever**—selling more than 400 million copies worldwide since it launched in 1997—it probably won't come as a surprise that J. K. Rowling's seven-book *Harry Potter* series is still riding high. The books have spawned eight movies, toys, video games, theme parks, and even a play—*Harry Potter and the Cursed Child*—scheduled to run in London, UK, in 2016.

3 DIVERGENT

From the same dystopian stable as series such as *The Maze Runner* and Suzanne Collins' *The Hunger Games*, Veronica Roth's *Divergent* trilogy explores a future society that is divided by personality types, as seen through the eyes of misfit Beatrice "Tris" Prior.

Roth shared the record for **highest earnings by a kids' author in 2014** with *Diary of a Wimpy Kid* writer Jeff Kinney (see no. 7): each achieving $17 million, as estimated by Forbes.

4 THE LAND OF STORIES

Glee actor Chris Colfer conceived this "modern-day fairy tale" at an early age as a way of escaping the real world. Following the adventures of twins Conner and Alex Bailey in an enchanted world, the series draws on many classic stories, including Cinderella, Goldilocks, and Peter Pan.

5 PERCY JACKSON

Rick Riordan's pentalogy *Percy Jackson and the Olympians* is the tale of teen Percy coming to terms with being a demigod—the son of Poseidon, no less. So plenty of big waves and thunderbolts are guaranteed. Percy also stars in the follow-up series *The Heroes of Olympus*, itself a best-seller.

6 THE GIVER

Proving that dystopia was popular among young readers long before 2015, the original *Giver* book, by Lois Lowry, was released in 1993. Set in a world where all emotion has been culled, it was followed by three books, plus its own feature film in 2014, starring Meryl Streep, Jeff Bridges, and Taylor Swift.

7 DIARY OF A WIMPY KID

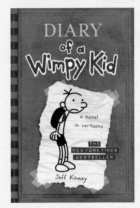

With more than 150 million copies in print, *Diary of a Wimpy Kid* by Jeff Kinney is by far the **most printed fictional kids' diary series**. Having made the transition from online, the series now boasts three tie-in movies and will see its 10th installment hit stores in November 2015.

8 THE KANIN CHRONICLES

Set in the icy world of her *Trylle* trilogy, Amanda Hocking's *Kanin Chronicles* follow tracker Bryn Aven as she seeks acceptance into her tribe, who are giving her the cold shoulder. Hocking's fifth series to date continues her trademark fantasy and paranormal themes.

9 THE SELECTION

Like *Divergent*'s "Tris", America Singer also lives in a fractured future society. Kiera Cass's series follows America's rise to the top, where she rubs shoulders with royalty. The fourth book, *The Heir*, was published in May 2015. There have also been four spin-off novellas.

10 DORK DIARIES

Hot on the heels of *Wimpy Kid* is the fictional journal series *Dork Diaries*, by Rachel Renée Russell—who is still proud to call herself a dork! With nine installments to date, these young teen books explore the everyday trials of 14-year-old Nikki Maxwell, visualized through humorous doodles and comic strips.

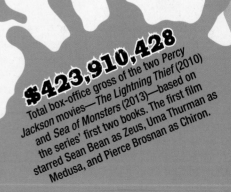

$423,910,428
Total box-office gross of the two Percy Jackson movies—*The Lightning Thief* (2010) and *Sea of Monsters* (2013)—based on the series' first two books. The first film starred Sean Bean as Zeus, Uma Thurman as Medusa, and Pierce Brosnan as Chiron.

TECHNOLOGY

TECH GO MOBILE

CALLING ALL RECORD-BREAKERS!

LARGEST GATHERING OF PEOPLE DRESSED AS CELL PHONES

Are you always on your phone? Well, for 275 people in San Juan, Puerto Rico, their phones were on *them* for this record! The army of cell phone dead ringers achieved the feat in an event organized by Open Mobile and Motorola in 2007, smashing the previous total of 194.

ACTUAL SIZE

THINNEST SMARTPHONE

Cell phones have certainly come a long way since the days of "The Brick" (see pp. 84–85), growing ever smaller and lighter. The slimmest cell phone to enter the market to date is the ELIFE S5.1 (left)—aka Gionee GN9005—measuring just 0.209 in (5.31 mm) at its widest point. Created by mobile manufacturer Gionee Communication Equipment, the slimline device was launched in China on September 4, 2014.

LARGEST SMARTPHONE ENSEMBLE

On June 15, 2013, an orchestra of 223 people played a tune with their smartphones, making use of virtual instruments via music apps. The performance was put on by students of the Beijing Contemporary Music Academy as part of the Vivo Xplay Mobile Music Festival, with some ambidexterous members even playing more than one device at the same time (inset).

FIRST DOG TO DETECT CELL PHONES

If you're the kind of person who's always misplacing their phone, you need a pooch like Murphy in your life. The smartphone-seeking springer-spaniel works with his handler, Mel Barker, to sniff out contraband items among inmates at Norwich Prison, UK. Murphy's nose is so atuned that he can even locate phones that have been hidden in wall cavities or wrapped in plastic bags.

HIGHEST CELL PHONE CALL

They say that if you're struggling to get reception you should head for higher ground. Well, British mountaineer Rod Baber took that advice to heart, and some! On May 21, 2007, he used his Motorola MOTO Z8 to make the highest-altitude, land-base call, from the peak of Everest, Earth's **highest mountain**, at a dizzying 29,029 ft (8,848 m).

While there, Baber also set a record for **highest text message**. It read: "One small step for man one giant step for mobilekind—thanks Motorola."

172,105,400
Sales of Apple's iPhone, the second best-selling smartphone brand in 2014 (based on the same Euromonitor International data), followed by Xiaomi, which shifted around 79,469,300 units.

WOW!

BEST-SELLING SMARTPHONE BRAND (CURRENT)

Samsung (South Korea) sold more smartphones in 2014 than any other brand—some 269,008,600 units—according to market research by Euromonitor International. The year 2015 saw the launch of its latest flagship handset, the Galaxy S6 (left), featuring an enhanced display and support for wireless charging.

TECH SUPER SCREENS

TINY TABLETS & MASSIVE MOVIE HOUSES

FIRST HANDHELD
TO SUPPORT GLASSES-FREE 3D

A long time ago, getting 3D effects at home meant having to wear special glasses. Then the Nintendo 3DS came along and changed everything. The popular handheld device created two images at once on a single screen, which the eyes viewed differently. This created the illusion of 3D. The console was launched in Japan on February 26, 2011.

BEST-SELLING TABLET OPERATING SYSTEM

Android is king of the operating systems, at least when it comes to sales. Approximately 122,925,000 tablets powered by the Google-developed OS sold in 2014, based on Euromonitor International data. That equates to 61.2% of the market, versus 32.6% claimed by devices using iOS.

And the records don't stop there for the little green robot … Android is also the **best-selling smartphone OS**, with some 883,083,000 handsets shifted in 2014.

TOP 5 TABLET SALES BY COUNTRY

1. USA
72,739,700

2. China
20,223,000

3. Russia
9,176,400

4. Brazil
8,020,900

5. Germany
6,756,500

Source: Euromonitor International, 2014

BEST-SELLING E-READER BRAND

Amazon's Kindle devices are currently the most popular for bookworms on the move. In 2014, the US company sold around 9,508,000 units, based on data from Euromonitor International. Kobo (Canada) was the second most popular e-reader series, with sales of 2,555,700.

LARGEST CINEMA SCREEN

In 1937, a temporary screen at the Paris Exposition in France stretched 297 ft (90.5 m) wide—almost as long as the Statue of Liberty is tall—and stood 32 ft 4 in (9.9 m) high. The **largest 35-mm movie-house screen**, meanwhile—showing movies shot on 35-mm film—is found at South Korea's Lotte Cinema (above). It measures 111 ft 9 in (34.07 m) long and 45 ft 4 in (13.84 m) high.

LARGEST 4K SCREEN AT A VIDEO-GAME COMPETITION

Attendees at Churchill Downs in Louisville, Kentucky, on September 9, 2014, got to see shooter game *Borderlands: The Pre-Sequel!* on a truly epic scale. Powered by NVIDIA's graphics-processing technology, the 4,000-pixel screen—15,224 sq ft (1,414.36 m²) in area—was impossible to miss.

BEST-SELLING TABLET BRAND

Launched in 2010, the Apple iPad has dominated the tablet market ever since. In 2014, shoppers snapped up some 65,167,900 iPads according to Euromonitor International research— almost double the 37,945,000 Samsung tablets sold.

With its multi-touch screen and multimedia functions, Apple's iPad is generally considered the first modern tablet. It has evolved over several generations, including the iPad 2 (left), iPad Mini, and iPad Air, with the release of the iPad Air 3 rumored for late 2015 or early 2016.

TECH WEARABLES

SMART GADGETS CLOSE TO HAND

BEST-SELLING WEARABLE ELECTRONICS BRAND

Wearable gadgets for tracking our exercise have picked up the pace in recent years. The current front-runner is Fitbit (USA), with some 11,794,000 units sold in 2014, based on Euromonitor International data. Fitbit's products, such as the wristbands above, are designed to gather data and relay it to other devices, e.g. a computer or a smartphone, for processing.

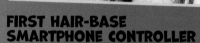

FIRST HAIR-BASE SMARTPHONE CONTROLLER

Brazilian inventor Katia Vega, who describes herself as a beauty technology designer, created Hairware as an innovative way of controlling personal technology such as cell phones. The conductive hair extensions (above) essentially let you control a phone by stroking your hair, with different gestures able to activate various apps/commands.

Vega has also invented a system that uses eyelid movements and conductive makeup as a method of controlling electronic devices. The technology was unveiled at a conference in 2013, where Katia demonstrated the **first drone launched by winking** (inset).

FIRST HAPTIC SHOES

This futuristic footwear is a form of wearable sat-nav. They direct you via gentle vibrations emitted from two "pods" (inset), which wirelessly connect to an associated app. Made by Indian company Lechal, the shoes were originally conceived as an aid for the visually impaired, but are equally useful for anyone who gets lost easily.

LARGEST COMPANY BY MARKET VALUE

In 2015, Forbes estimated Apple to be worth $741.8 billion in terms of market value—putting it way ahead of second-place Google on $367.6 billion.

Adding to its ever-growing tech portfolio, the company took its first step into wearables in 2015 with the release of the Apple Watch (left). Sales forecasts already suggest it is topping the smartwatch field.

FIRST HAPTIC JACKET USED FOR NAVIGATION

If your shoes aren't giving you enough haptic feedback, the Navigate Jacket, made by wearable tech company We:eX (USA/ Australia), could be the perfect solution—as long as you're only exploring Paris, New York, or Sydney. The cutting-edge coat uses a mix of haptic feedback and LED lights to subtly guide you through the three cities. It steers you toward your final destination—preset via a companion app—by vibrating whenever you need to turn.

MOST MONEY PLEDGED FOR A HAPTIC DEVICE ON KICKSTARTER

Designed by technology innovator Immerz (USA), the KOR-FX vest is designed for gamers who want to experience the action as physically as possible. The vest allows them to feel the impact of every in-game punch, gunshot or explosion through real-time feedback. By July 24, 2014, the KOR-FX had raised $183,449 in funding.

MOST MONEY PLEDGED FOR A KICKSTARTER PROJECT

No other project on the world's **largest crowdfunding platform** (see pp. 156–57) has attracted more pledges than the Pebble smartwatch, which syncs with both iOS and Android devices. When the initial funding period closed on May 18, 2012, it had reached $10,266,845 from 68,929 backers; by September 9, 2015 this had risen to $20,338,986.

WOW!

28:56
4.08mi
PACE
7:05
min/mi

twelve thirty five

TUE 27

TECH RETRO TECH

LOOKING BACK AT THE FIRST ...

CELL PHONE CALL
The *concept* of a portable telephone first appeared in 1947 at Lucent Technologies' Bell Labs in New Jersey. The first *actual* portable telephone handset, however, was invented by Martin Cooper (USA, left), of Motorola, who made the first call on April 3, 1973. This first ever cellular call was made to Cooper's rival, Joel Engel, head of research at Bell Labs!

CLAMSHELL LAPTOP
Regarded as the first "true" laptop, the GRiD Compass was designed in 1979 by William Moggridge (UK) for GRiD Systems Corporation (USA). It was introduced in 1982 with a RAM of 512K. It weighed 11 lb (5 kg) and cost a whopping $10,000—equivalent to $24,500 in today's money! This didn't stop NASA from ordering GRiD laptops for use on the Space Shuttle in the early 1980s.

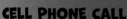

1964   1973   1975   1979   1982

COMPUTER MOUSE
The mouse—as in the computer peripheral, not the rodent—was invented by Douglas Engelbart (USA) in 1964 (and patented in the USA in 1970). Originally made from wood, it was described as an "X-Y position indicator for a display system," and was nicknamed a mouse because of the resemblance of the wire to a tail.

DIGITAL CAMERA
Steve Sasson (USA) of Kodak built a prototype digital camera in 1975. It weighed 8 lb (3.6 kg)— about the same as an adult human head—and was the size of a toaster. It took black-and-white images with a resolution of 0.01 megapixels, and used a cassette of magnetic tape as its on-board storage medium.

EMOTICON
The first "smiley" was used by Scott Fahlman (USA) of Carnegie Mellon University, Pittsburgh, on September 19, 1982. In a message on a bulletin-board system, he proposed the use of :-) and :-(in e-mails to signify the emotional context of the message.

$3,995

Cost of the DynaTAC cell phone in 1985—equal to $8,790 in today's money. Despite the cost, there was a six-month waiting list when it first went on sale.

COMMERCIALLY AVAILABLE PC WITH A GRAPHICAL USER INTERFACE

In 1984, Apple Macintosh released its first computer, complete with an 8-MHz processor and 128 KB of memory. It became the first popular PC to feature a graphical user interface (GUI), as opposed to command line (text-only interface).

1983

ACTUAL SIZE

1984   1987

COMMERCIALLY AVAILABLE CELL PHONE

The DynaTAC 8000X went on sale on March 6, 1983. Made by Motorola, it weighed in at a hefty 27.69 oz (785 g)—six times heavier than an iPhone 6—and measured 13 x 1.75 x 3.5 in (330 x 44 x 89 mm). It's not surprising that its creators affectionately nicknamed it "The Brick." It took 10 hours to charge it up for 30 minutes of call time.

JPEG

The JPEG was developed by the Joint Photographic Experts Group in Copenhagen, Denmark, in order to standardize how images are compressed for use on the Internet and in digital cameras. The first JPEGs created by the group—on June 18, 1987— were a set of four test images called "Barbara" (above left), "Boats" (above right), "Toys," and "Zelda."

MOTOROLA DYNA T·A·C 8000X

TECH

GET CODING

DO YOU SPEAK COMPUTER?

MOST PEOPLE TRAINED IN COMPUTER PROGRAMMING IN EIGHT HOURS

When it comes to computing, Microsoft needs no introductions, but as well as making computer software, the company is also heavily involved in *training* the next generation of potential computer scientists. At the 2015 Microsoft Imagine Coding Camp, 1,337 pupils from Washington state received eight hours of coding tuition for free.

OLDEST PROGRAMMING LANGUAGE STILL IN USE

It was a few years after the invention of computers that anything resembling a programming language appeared. However, because a lot of the earlier systems work differently to those used today, most of them are no longer in operation. FORTRAN is a major exception.

Developed originally by IBM for coding its 704 mainframe computer (above), FORTRAN was released in April 1957 and has been continually developed for 58 years and counting; its last major update was in 2010. It's incredible to think that in its early days, before the arrival of disk drives or terminals, lines of code were created and stored on punched-out cards (right)—a practice used until the 1980s.

MOST PEOPLE IN A SOFTWARE DEVELOPMENT MARATHON

Kids aren't the only ones getting involved in en-masse coding at Microsoft (see above left)—grown-ups are at it, too! During a special event to mark the launch of Windows 8 in 2012, a total of 2,567 Microsoft employees came together in Bangalore, India, for 18 hours of nonstop app development for the new platform.

MOST RASPBERRY PIs OPERATING IN PARALLEL

A single Raspberry Pi is powerful enough for most computing tasks, but imagine what more than one could do … Online coding platform Resin.io decided to find out by connecting 120 Raspberry Pis to create a sort of "supercomputer" to test their new website. Their Pi tower, renamed as "The Beast," was revealed on October 6, 2014, along with a request for ideas for future uses of the Pi cluster. Suggestions to date include a gaming interface and a weather mapper.

HIGHEST FREEFALL BY A TEDDY BEAR

Inspired by Felix Baumgartner (see p. 170), the Raspberry Pi Foundation and balloonist Dave Akerman sent Raspberry Pi mascot Babbage the Bear into the sky, attached to a Pi-controlled weather balloon.

Taking off on August 24, 2013, the intrepid bear was meant to reach 24.2 miles (39 km), but—due to an electrical fault—Babbage rose to 25.48 miles (41 km) before the balloon burst. A second attempt two days later saw Babbage reach the intended altitude, at which point his parachute deployed and he began his heroic descent back to Earth (right).

WOW!

5 MILLION

Raspberry Pis sold as of February 2015, since being launched in 2012. As the Raspberry Pi Foundation is a charity, all its profits go back into R&D and educational initiatives, such as the "Picademy" for teachers.

INSIDE THE RASPBERRY PI

Considering that this compact computer is no bigger than a credit card, it sure packs in a lot of features, including Ethernet, HDMI, and USB ports, plus audio, camera, and display interfaces. Released in early 2015, the second-generation Raspberry Pi (B+ pictured) boasts an even higher spec than the original, with a 900-MHz quad-core CPU and 1GB of RAM. The fact that all this is available for just $35 makes it the perfect starter device for aspiring computer scientists.

4 USB slots for mouse, keyboard, etc.

40 GPIO pins to connect to other devices

Ethernet port links to the internet

CPU, GPU, and RAM are found in this microchip

Combined video and audio jack

HDMI for linking to a digital TV or monitor

Slot for SD cards (underneath)

Power is received via a microUSB, like a cell phone

TECH 3D PRINTING

CHANGING THE WORLD, LAYER BY LAYER

FIRST 3D-PRINTED CAR

It took 44 hours of printing in layers—spread over five days in September 2014—to create *Strati*, the first car to have both its chassis and its body 3D-printed (detail inset). It was the brainchild of crowd-funded Local Motors, based in Phoenix, Arizona, who completed the car's design with help from Oak Ridge National Laboratory and manufacturing company SABIC.

WOW!

FIRST VILLAGE TO 3D-PRINT ALL OF ITS RESIDENTS

In Spain, all 318 residents of the village of Torrequebradilla have been scanned and printed out in full-color 3D. The project was created by the Spanish company Grupo Sicnova, who did all the scanning in a single day. Grupo Sicnova hope to one day scan and print 3D models for every person in Spain. The company used its new CloneScan 3D machine—a 7-ft-tall (2.13-m) body scanner—to complete 90-second-long scans of each person. Each of the scanned residents received their own miniature clone within a week of the scanning event (inset).

FIRST 3D-PRINTED DRESS

It's now possible to buy an entire ready-to-wear, one-piece dress straight from the printer. In September 2014, Nervous System of Massachusetts created a design program called "Kinematics" to produce the completely flexible outfit (right).

The use of 3D-printed fabrics, however, dates back as far as 1999/2000. This is when Dutch industrial engineers led by Jiri Evenhuis created the **first dress made from 3D-printed fabric**. The Drape Dress was "knitted" together from interlocking rings of 3D-printed nylon (inset), a little like plastic chain mail.

FIRST OBJECT 3D-PRINTED IN SPACE

Got into orbit, then realized you've left your spanner at home? Don't worry, you can now just print one! In 2014, NASA and tech company Made in Space (USA) proved that this could work by sending a 3D printer to the *International Space Station*. There, on November 24, 2014, astronauts printed off a spare part for the printer itself. Pictured above is *ISS* Commander Barry "Butch" Wilmore holding the extruder plate, which carried the NASA and MiS logos.

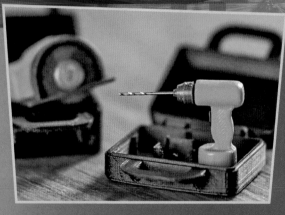

SMALLEST WORKING POWER TOOL

Lance Abernethy from Auckland, New Zealand, uses 3D-printing technology to manufacture miniature power tools. Pictured left at actual size is Lance's most petite power tool: a 3D-printed cordless drill that's just 0.66 in (17 mm) tall and holds a 0.019-in-wide (0.5-mm) drill bit. In the picture above, you can also see his minuscule circular saw, which measures a mere 0.56 in (14.3 mm) in length and is fitted with a 0.47-in (12-mm) working blade.

ACTUAL SIZE

FIRST 3D-PRINTED BIONIC EAR

In May 2013, nanotechnology scientists at Princeton University, in collaboration with Johns Hopkins University (both USA), used a commercially available printer to create a bionic ear. The ear was printed from a type of gel known as "hydrogel," mixed with cow cells and a plastic containing silver particles. For now, the appendage can only pick up radio signals, but scientists hope to one day be able to create a similar ear that can detect sounds.

TECH DRONES

TECHNOLOGY TAKES OFF

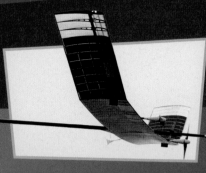

FIRST PHONE-CONTROLLED FLYING MACHINE

The *AR.Drone* is a hovering, rotor-power device which was designed and built in 2010 by the French company Parrot. A quadcopter (i.e., it has four rotors), it can be controlled using an iPad, iPod, or iPhone and used to play AR (augmented reality) games. An on-board camera allows the player to see the landscape from the device's point of view, making it easier to target virtual enemies.

HIGHEST ALTITUDE BY A CIVIL DRONE AIRCRAFT

Zephyr is a high-altitude, long-endurance (HALE) drone that was test-flown over Dubai in the United Arab Emirates on September 11, 2014. The unmanned craft reached an altitude of 61,696 ft (18,805 m)—the highest for a civilian (i.e., nonmilitary) drone flight. How high is this? It's twice the height of Mount Everest—the world's **highest mountain**!

40.2 MPH

Top speed of DHL's *Paketcopter* (below)—equal to 59 ft (18 m) per second—depending on wind strength. It flies at an altitude of around 164 ft (50 m), with an upper limit of 328 ft (100 m).

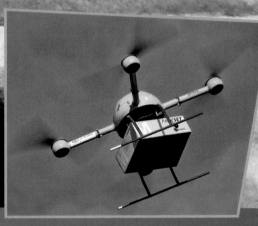

FIRST COMMERCIAL TRANSPORT DRONE

Having your online shopping delivered by drone might soon be a reality, thanks to global shipping company DHL. Their *Paketcopter*, aka *Parcelcopter*, had its first successful test in Germany in December 2013, when medicine was flown across the city of Bonn from a pharmacy to DHL headquarters. The first scheduled service will see the *Paketcopter* deliver medicines and other urgent supplies to the German island of Juist in the North Sea.

MOST ACCURATE 3D MODEL OF CHRIST THE REDEEMER

It took almost a decade (1922–31) to build the original Christ the Redeemer statue—the giant statue of Jesus that stands at the top of Corcovado Mountain in Rio de Janeiro, Brazil (above). In February 2015, it took just six days to re-create the statue digitally, in 3D (inset below), using drone technology. Software specialist Pix4D, PUC University of Rio de Janeiro, and Canadian UAV maker Aeryon used quadcopters equipped with cameras to snap 2,090 separate photographs (main image). These were then sewn together and mapped to the model, which was composed from 2.5 million triangles.

WOW!

LONGEST FLIGHT IN SPACE BY A DRONE

Drones come in all shapes and sizes, and the larger ones have now escaped the confines of Earth. The Boeing X-37B "Orbital Test Vehicle" (OTV) is an unmanned US Air Force spacecraft that looks like the *Space Shuttle*. On October 17, 2014, the third mission of the X-37B returned to Earth after spending nearly 675 days in orbit around the planet. The OTV landed at Vandenberg Air Force Base in California after carrying out a range of secret experiments and observations from orbit.

CHALLENGE

PICTURE YOURSELF AS A RECORD-BREAKER!

LONGEST RELAY CHAIN OF SELFIES

Here's a chance to snap your way into the *Guinness World Records* books. All you need is a camera-enabled tablet or smartphone … that, and a few hundred friends!

The challenge here is to form a really long line of people taking selfies. But each participant must take it in turn to snap a selfie with the person next to them. So, person No. 1 takes a selfie with person No. 2, No. 2 then takes one with No. 3, No. 3 with No. 4, and so on.

You'll need to beat the current record of 531, so perhaps your school or after-school club might want to have a go? Say "cheese!"

FIRST SELFIE ...

... in space	Michael Collins (USA)	July 18, 1966
... while spacewalking	Edwin "Buzz" Aldrin (USA)	November 13, 1966
... on another planet	*Curiosity* rover on Mars	October 31, 2012

BUZZ ALDRIN

CURIOSITY ROVER

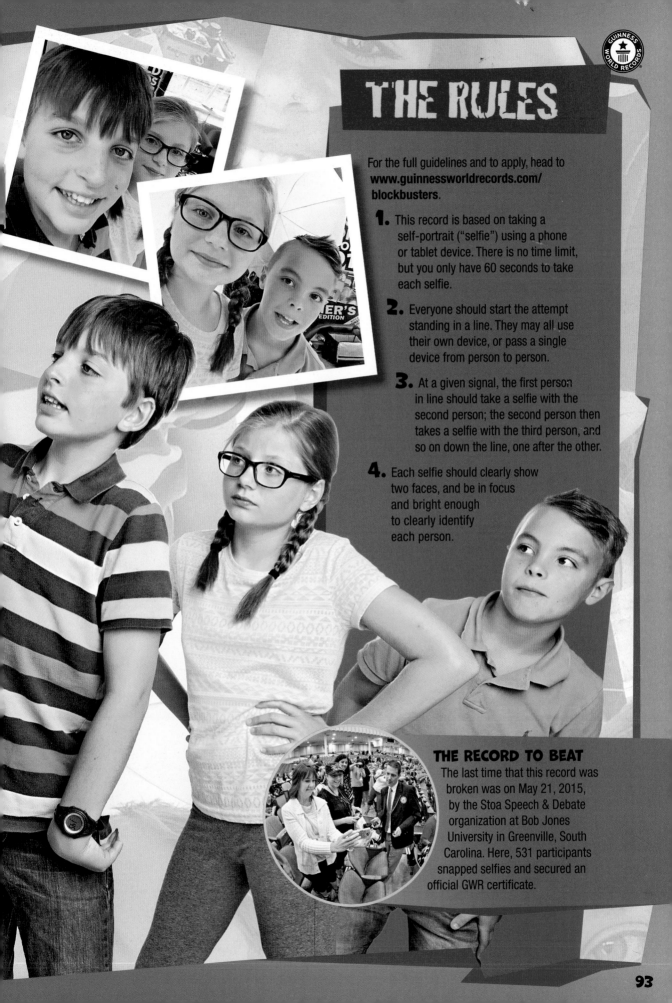

THE RULES

For the full guidelines and to apply, head to **www.guinnessworldrecords.com/blockbusters**.

1. This record is based on taking a self-portrait ("selfie") using a phone or tablet device. There is no time limit, but you only have 60 seconds to take each selfie.

2. Everyone should start the attempt standing in a line. They may all use their own device, or pass a single device from person to person.

3. At a given signal, the first person in line should take a selfie with the second person; the second person then takes a selfie with the third person, and so on down the line, one after the other.

4. Each selfie should clearly show two faces, and be in focus and bright enough to clearly identify each person.

THE RECORD TO BEAT

The last time that this record was broken was on May 21, 2015, by the Stoa Speech & Debate organization at Bob Jones University in Greenville, South Carolina. Here, 531 participants snapped selfies and secured an official GWR certificate.

TECH ROBOTS

RESISTANCE IS FUTILE

FARTHEST DISTANCE COVERED BY A QUADRUPED ROBOT

BigDog, developed by Boston Dynamics (USA), is a four-legged robot designed to be a "pack mule" for soldiers traveling on rough terrain. In February 2009, the developers announced that BigDog had walked 12.8 miles (20.5 km) without any support other than GPS tracking.

MOST AGILE HUMANOID ROBOT

Meet Atlas, the humanlike robot that can run over rocky terrain and stay upright—even when hit with a 20-lb (9-kg) medicine ball! He was built by the US company Boston Dynamics, which makes robots for the US military. Atlas is bipedal (has two legs) and has upper limbs that can lift and carry weights as it walks.

FIRST COMPANION ROBOT IN SPACE

Kirobo is a robot astronaut designed as a companion for Koichi Wakata—Japan's first commander of the *International Space Station* (*ISS*). On December 7, 2013, while the *ISS* was 257 miles (414 km) above Earth's sea level, Kirobo and Wakata had a face-to-face conversation (above)—the **highest altitude for a robot conversation**.

MOST LIFELIKE ANDROID

Making robots that look like us is almost as difficult as making them *think* like us. Even so, in March 2011, Osaka University and Japanese robotics company Kokoro unveiled the lifelike robot Geminoid DK. The android is constructed in the likeness of technology professor Henrik Schärfe of Denmark, and can achieve convincing gestures and facial expressions. Can you tell which one is human?

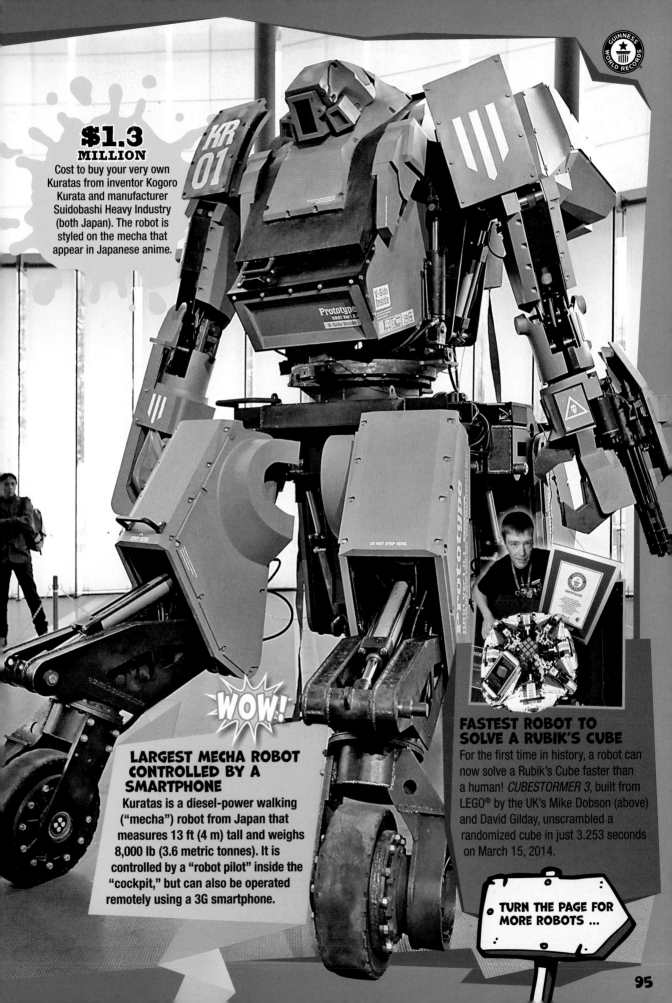

$1.3 MILLION

Cost to buy your very own Kuratas from inventor Kogoro Kurata and manufacturer Suidobashi Heavy Industry (both Japan). The robot is styled on the mecha that appear in Japanese anime.

WOW!

LARGEST MECHA ROBOT CONTROLLED BY A SMARTPHONE

Kuratas is a diesel-power walking ("mecha") robot from Japan that measures 13 ft (4 m) tall and weighs 8,000 lb (3.6 metric tonnes). It is controlled by a "robot pilot" inside the "cockpit," but can also be operated remotely using a 3G smartphone.

FASTEST ROBOT TO SOLVE A RUBIK'S CUBE

For the first time in history, a robot can now solve a Rubik's Cube faster than a human! *CUBESTORMER 3*, built from LEGO® by the UK's Mike Dobson (above) and David Gilday, unscrambled a randomized cube in just 3.253 seconds on March 15, 2014.

TURN THE PAGE FOR MORE ROBOTS ...

TECH ROBOTS

RISE OF THE MACHINES!

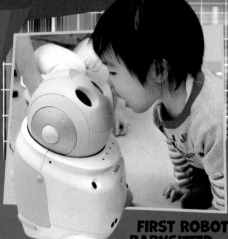

FIRST ROBOT BABYSITTER

"Partner-type Personal Robots," aka PaPeRos, are a range of prototype helper bots for the home developed by Japanese tech giant NEC. Beyond the series' advanced communication skills and obstacle detection, the Childcare PaPeRo also features built-in TV conferencing so that parents can check in on their child via the droid's camera eyes and microphones.

FASTEST ROBOT JOCKEY

The traditional Middle Eastern sport of camel racing saw a 21st-century twist with the introduction of robotic riders. Initially developed by Swiss company K-Team, Kamel (above) was given a humanlike face and jockey colors to avoid spooking the animals. The shock-proof robots, which can stay atop a camel at speeds of up to 25 mph (40 km/h), are remote-controlled by technicians from vehicles driving alongside the track.

3,000

Words in PaPeRo's vocabulary, enabling it to interact with humans. It can recognize up to 30 faces, too, so it should know exactly who it's talking to!

FIRST ROBOT TRUMPETER

If you've ever tried to play a brass instrument, you'll know it's no easy task, demanding complex movements of the mouth and fingers. One member of a robot "band" created by Toyota was engineered to play the trumpet like a pro, with vibrating lips and piston-powered fingers.

FIRST RESTAURANT WITH ROBOT WAITERS

Ever been served by someone acting like an automaton? Well, at the Robot Kitchen in Hong Kong, China, robotic service is guaranteed, with two droids taking your order and serving food—all with an unflappable LED smile. The pioneering diner has since inspired further robot restaurants and even a hotel (see opposite).

FIRST ROBOT-STAFFED HOTEL

One minute they're terrifying the visitors to *Jurassic World*, the next they're answering your enquiries at a hotel reception. Is there no end to Velociraptors' talents? Opening on July 16, 2015, in Nagasaki, Japan, Henn-na Hotel ("Strange Hotel") certainly lives up to its name. In addition to the robo-dino, three humanoid androids, known as "actroids," greet customers at reception, while a mechanical porter sorts out luggage. Other bots at the hotel perform domestic duties, such as cleaning rooms and serving coffee.

MOST THERAPEUTIC ROBOT

PARO the seal might look supercute, but he's no toy; his job is to keep patients calm. Invented by Takanori Shibata of the Intelligent Systems Research Institute in Japan, PARO's built-in sensors allow him to respond to light, sound, and touch. A six-week trial at a day-care center for the elderly showed that residents had a marked increase in a natural chemical, called 17-KS-S, produced by the body when relaxed. PARO certainly gets the GWR *seal* of approval!

WOW!

FIRST ROBOT HAND TO PROVIDE REAL-TIME FEEDBACK

Dennis Aabo Sørensen of Denmark (right) lost his hand in a fireworks accident in 2005. On February 5, 2014, a team of scientists—headed up by the École Polytechnique Fédérale de Lausanne in Switzerland—made a great leap in robotics and prosthetics technology by providing Dennis with a robotic hand wired into the nerves in his upper arm. Wearing a blindfold and earplugs, Dennis could respond to the instant feedback from the prosthesis by distinguishing between various objects' shapes and rigidity, and adjusting his grip accordingly.

TECH ROBOTS

MONSTER ROBOTICS ON A LARGE "SCALE"

Ability to breathe fire

Height: 26 ft

Weight: 12.1 tons

Length: 51 ft

DAMSEL IN DISTRESS!!!!!

4,265 FEET
of electrical cabling to provide
Fanny with power.

5,579 FL OZ
of oil to operate Fanny's
hydraulic systems.

40-ft-wide
flappable wings

Moving joints controlled by
272 valves, 50 hydraulic drives,
and 5,579 fl oz of lubricant

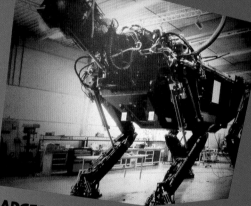

LARGEST WALKING ROBOT

Meet Fanny, the 12.1-ton (11-metric-tonne) dragon
from Zandt in Germany. Fanny proves that robots
aren't just industrial machines on production lines.
You can build your own robot from scratch in your
garage! That's what Zollner Electronik did in 2012
to bring this huge beast to life.

Measuring 51 ft 6 in (15.72 m) long by 26 ft 10 in
(8 m) tall, Fanny is a radio-controlled robot dragon
powered by a 2.0-liter turbo diesel engine. The
mighty mechatronic beast (pictured above without
its scaly covering) is radio remote-controlled and
was created for Germany's longest-running folk play.

Legs with seven degrees of
motion, allowing Fanny to walk to
the side and also around corners

Walks on all fours at
a speed of 1.1 mph

TECH TOP 10

BEST-SELLING GAMES CONSOLES

Listed here are the biggest-selling games consoles of all time, as calculated by VGChartz. Just three manufacturers appear on the list: Nintendo (five entries), Sony (four), and Microsoft (one). While it's a Sony console in the No. 1 spot, Nintendo has enjoyed more sales from its five entries in the top 10—518 million compared with Sony's 428 million. So, in the battle of the consoles, you could say it's a draw …

DID YOU KNOW?
During the Thanksgiving period in 2002, the Game Boy Advance became the **first console to sell 1 million units in 10 days.**

10

61.91 million

NINTENDO ENTERTAINMENT SYSTEM
The NES was released in Japan in 1983 (as the Famicom) and in North America in 1985; it saw the debut of series such as *Super Mario Bros.*, *The Legend of Zelda*, *Metroid*, and *Final Fantasy*.

9

80.82 million

PLAYSTATION PORTABLE
One of the stars of E3 2004 was Sony's seventh-generation handheld console. With its video player and TV tuner, the PSP finally offered some serious competition against Nintendo's domination, and was more powerful than its closest rival, the DS (see right).

8

81.51 million

GAME BOY ADVANCE
The sixth-generation GBA was launched by Nintendo in 2001 and dominated the market until the launch of its successor, the DS, in 2004; its biggest-selling title was *Pokémon Ruby and Sapphire*, with sales of 16 million copies.

7

84.9 million

XBOX 360
Microsoft's contender in the battle for seventh-generation supremacy was the successor to the original Xbox. Released in 2005, the 360's biggest selling point was its online gaming and digital media features.

6

85.83 million

PLAYSTATION 3
Sony's PS3 launched in 2006 to excitable gamers—fans fought over the chance to be first to buy it, going as far as shooting fellow shoppers or robbing them at gunpoint! As the first console to use Blu-ray discs, the PS3 just got the edge over its rival, the Xbox 360, although was beaten to the top of the seventh-gen chart by the Wii (right).

1.5 BILLION

Games sold to PlayStation 2 owners, according to GameSpot; 3,874 different titles were published—an average sale of 387,196 per title!

1

2

3

4

5

157.68 million

PLAYSTATION 2
The PS2 (2000) reigned supreme for more than a decade as the world's favorite console. It also secured the record for the **fastest games console to ship 100 million units**, doing so in 5 years 9 months—three years faster than its predecessor, the PS1 (see left). It was superceded by the PS3 in 2006, but such was its popularity that it was still being produced as late as 2013.

154.88 million

NINTENDO DS
The world's **best-selling handheld games console**, the DS debuted in 2004 with tandem screens, wi-fi connectivity, and an in-built microphone. Contributing to its success was the fact that it was backward compatible with the Game Boy Advance, making the DS a natural successor to the Game Boy series.

118.69 million

GAME BOY
In 1989, Nintendo launched their pocket-size Game Boy—and its bundled game *Tetris*—kicking off a revolution in handheld gaming. More than 450 titles gave gamers plenty to choose from, so no wonder this powerful little console took the world by storm.

104.25 million

PLAYSTATION
The PS1 was released in Japan in 1994 and North America and Europe in 1995, and—9.5 years later—became the **first console to sell 100 million units**. The PS1 also heralded the beginning of the end for cartridge-base home consoles such as the NES and N64.

101.17 million

Wii
The Wii—Nintendo's smallest home console to date—was promoted on its family-friendly gaming and broad user appeal; it obviously worked, appealing to kids and grandparents alike and outselling the PS3 and Xbox 360. It didn't have the lasting appeal that its rivals had, though, and it was discontinued in October 2013.

? DID YOU KNOW?

The **best-selling game on the PS2** is *Grand Theft Auto: San Andreas*, with 20.81 million copies sold as of September 18, 2015.

MUSIC

SOLO ARTISTS

RECORD-BREAKING FEMALES IN POP

FASTEST-SELLING ALBUM ON iTUNES

In December 2013, Beyoncé (USA) took the music industry and her own fans by surprise when she released, unannounced, her *Beyoncé* album as an iTunes exclusive. The unusual move paid off. In its first three days of availability as a download, the "visual" album—featuring 14 new tracks and 17 videos—shifted 828,773 copies worldwide. This shattered the iTunes record by Justin Timberlake's *The 20/20 Experience* (580,000), set earlier in 2013.

BIGGEST-SELLING DIGITAL SINGLE

"Call Me Maybe," by Canadian singer-songwriter Carly Rae Jepsen, has sold an estimated 15.1 million copies worldwide since its 2011 release. The supercatchy, Grammy-nominated single was a global Top 5 smash and hit the No. 1 spot in 19 countries, including the USA, Canada, Australia, France, South Korea, Venezuela, and the UK.

MOST NICKELODEON KIDS' CHOICE AWARDS WON BY A FEMALE

Selena Gomez (USA) has claimed a total of nine trophies at the Nickelodeon Kids' Choice Awards. She won five consecutive "Favorite TV Actress" awards (2009–13) for playing Alex Russo in the TV sitcom *Wizards of Waverly Place*, three "Favorite Female Singer" gongs (2012, 2014–15), and a 2014 trophy for "Best Fan Army" ("Selenators"). The only person with more awards is actor Will Smith, with 10.

MOST US NO. 1 SINGLES IN A YEAR BY A FEMALE

In 2010, Barbados-born singer Rihanna became the only female artist to have four US Hot 100 No. 1 singles within one calendar year: "Rude Boy," "Love the Way You Lie" (featuring Eminem), "What's My Name?" (featuring Drake), and "Only Girl (In the World)."

Rihanna also achieved the **most No. 1 singles on the US Digital Songs chart**, with 13. Those tracks spent a cumulative total of 38 weeks at the top spot.

WOW!

HIGHEST ANNUAL EARNINGS FOR A FEMALE POP STAR

According to Forbes, Katy Perry (USA) earned a whopping $135 million in the 12 months to June 2015. On the "Highest-Paid Celebrities" list, the singer was ranked third behind boxers Floyd Mayweather ($300 million) and Manny Pacquiao ($160 million).

Perry holds many other world records, including **most viewed music video online by a female artist**: "Dark Horse" had a VEVO viewer count of 1,033,932,849 as of July 25, 2015. The video features the supertalented Jiff the dog (right), who has set two records of his own—**fastest 5 m on front paws by a dog** and **fastest 10 m on hind legs by a dog.**

118.5 MILLION
Estimated number of viewers who watched Katy Perry's epic performance at the Super Bowl XLIX Halftime Show on February 1, 2015 (pictured), according to Nielsen.

MOST MILLION-SELLING WEEKS ON THE US ALBUMS CHART

Taylor Swift (USA) is the only singer to boast three albums that have surpassed 1 million sales in a week, since Nielsen SoundScan started tracking sales in 1991. She set this record with first-week sales of her third, fourth, and fifth studio albums: *Speak Now* (1.047 million), *Red* (1.208 million), and *1989* (1.287 million). Swift work indeed!

SOLO ARTISTS

RECORD-BREAKING MALES IN POP

HIGHEST EVER EARNINGS FOR A MUSICIAN

In the 12 months to June 2014, rapper Dr. Dre achieved a pretax income of $620 million, as estimated by Forbes. This dwarfs 2015's **top-earning musician**, Katy Perry (USA), with a $135-million income.

BEST-SELLING ALBUM EVER

Released back in 1982, Michael Jackson's (USA, 1958–2009) album *Thriller* remains unsurpassed in terms of sales to this day. Figures vary, but it has shifted some 65 million copies worldwide.

Although Jackson passed away in 2009, demand for his music shows no sign of abating. In October 2014, Forbes estimated the King of Pop's annual income to be $140 million, making him the **highest-earning dead celebrity**.

MOST HOT 100 ENTRIES BY A SOLO ARTIST

As of August 8, 2015, rapper Lil Wayne had placed 126 songs on the *Billboard* Hot 100. His debut was "Back that Thang Up" in 1999 and his 126th entry, "How Many Times," debuted at No. 74 on May 30, 2015.

To date, he has appeared on the Hot 100 as lead artist 45 times and 81 times as a featured artist.

MOST "LIKED" DJ ON FACEBOOK

Best known for his chart-topping collaborations and remixes, including "Titanium" (2011), "Without You" (2011), and "Hey Mama" (2015), French DJ David Guetta is as popular online as he is on the dance floor, with a whopping 55,723,936 "likes" for his Facebook profile as of July 27, 2015.

Proving that he is no one-hit wonder on social media, Guetta also holds the title for **most followed DJ on Twitter**, with 18,151,830 followers as of the same date on his @davidguetta page.

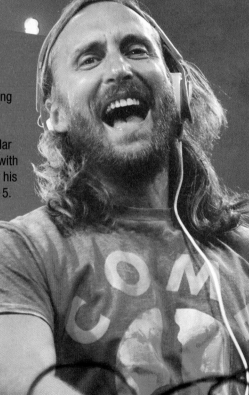

YOUNGEST ARTIST TO ACHIEVE FIVE NO. 1 ALBUMS

With *Believe Acoustic*, released in January 2013, Justin Bieber (Canada, b. March 1, 1994) achieved his fifth US No. 1 before his 19th birthday.

Bieber can also boast the **most Nickelodeon Kids' Choice Awards for a male singer**, with four. In 2011 he won "Favorite Song" (for "Baby") and in 2011–13 he won in the "Favorite Singer" category. At the 2012 ceremony, he got more than he bargained for on stage (inset).

4,895,505

"Dislikes" for Justin Bieber's song "Baby" on YouTube, as of July 27, 2015—the **most "disliked" video online**. No one ever said that being a pop star was going to be all plain sailing!

57,607

First-week sales of "The A-Team", the debut single by Ed Sheeran. In December 2013, it received a "Song of the Year" Grammy nomination, although the actual award was won by "We Are Young" by Fun featuring Janelle Monáe.

WOW!

MOST CONSECUTIVE WEEKS IN UK TOP 40

"Thinking Out Loud," by British singer-songwriter Ed Sheeran, made its debut in the UK's Official Singles Chart on July 5, 2014 and enjoyed its 54th consecutive week in the Top 40 on July 11, 2015.

Sheeran has had a warm reception across the Atlantic, too. The ballad peaked at No. 2 on the Hot 100 on January 31, 2015, and the No. 1 album from which it comes—*x*—had notched up an impressive 62 weeks on the *Billboard* 200, as of September 12, 2015.

MUSIC GROUPS

BANDING TOGETHER TO REACH NO. 1

MOST CUMULATIVE WEEKS ON THE HOT 100 (ONE SINGLE)

Nevada rockers Imagine Dragons hit the big time with their single "Radioactive," the opener on their debut album *Night Visions*. The song spent an incredible 87 nonconsecutive weeks in the US Hot 100 singles chart between August 18, 2012, and May 10, 2014.

MOST WEEKS AT NO. 1 ON THE US ALTERNATIVE SONGS CHART

"Madness" by British rock band Muse topped the Billboard Alternative Songs countdown for 19 weeks from October 13, 2012, surpassing the Foo Fighters' 18 weeks with their single "The Pretender." In 2015, "Dead Inside" became Muse's fourth Alternative Songs No. 1, taking their tally of cumulative No. 1 weeks to 45. Muse's frontman Matthew Bellamy (above) is famed for his epic vocal range, but this feat has to be a serious high note for the group.

BIGGEST-SELLING COUNTRY DIGITAL SONG

"Bro-country" duo Florida Georgia Line, aka Brian Kelley and Tyler Hubbard, didn't hang about in their quest to hit the top. The talented pair exploded onto the music scene in 2012 with their first single—"Cruise"—which has since become the most downloaded country track. As of April 2015, the upbeat anthem had shifted 7.24 million digital copies. Sales of the track were also boosted by a remix featuring rapper Nelly.

BIGGEST-SELLING DIGITAL SINGLE BY A GROUP

Released in 2009, "I Gotta Feeling" by The Black Eyed Peas is one of the hip-hoppers' most popular tracks. It has sold an estimated 15 million copies worldwide, including 8.7 million in the USA alone. It also spent 14 consecutive weeks at No. 1 in the Hot 100. Did will.i.am and co. *have a feeling* that it would do so well?

FIRST ACT TO DEBUT AT US NO. 1 WITH THEIR FIRST FOUR ALBUMS

It didn't take long for America to take One Direction to its heart. The British boy band scored a quadruplet of No. 1s with their first four albums. *Up All Night* (2011), *Take Me Home* (2012), *Midnight Memories* (2013), and *Four* (2014) all took the top spot on the Billboard 200. As we went to press, the group's future looked uncertain. The shock departure of Zayn (above middle) in early 2015 was followed by an announcement in August that the group would be taking a break.

WOW!

BEAT THIS!

FEEL THE RHYTHM, MAKE SOME NOISE

WOW!

LARGEST DRUM KIT

Named "The Big Boom," this dizzying drum set would require a pair of seriously long arms to play! Created by the Austrian group Drumartic, the kit is the world's largest in terms of size dimensions. It's a 5.2:1-scale replica of a pro kit, with each piece sized in proportion to its regular-size equivalent. The quartet not only presented the kit for measuring in Lienz, Austria, on October 7, 2012, but also gave it a bash!

MOST PIECES IN A DRUM KIT

When Dr. Mark Temperato of New York sits down to play the drums, you have to wonder how he knows what to hit next. His epic drum kit took 20 years to assemble and is comprised of 813 individual pieces, including multiple snares, tom-toms, cowbells, and cymbals.

Dr. Temperato works as a church reverend and tours as a drummer under his stage name "RevM." Incredibly, every piece in his set is playable from a single seated position. Dr. Temperato's record was verified on March 21, 2013, smashing his own count of 340 pieces from 2011.

LARGEST DRUM

If you want to make a noise, then try giving this hefty tub a thump! It measures 18 ft 2 in (5.54 m) in diameter, stands at 19 ft 6 in (5.96 m) tall, and weighs in at 15,432 lb (7,000 kg). It was created by the Yeongdong-gun local government and Lee Seuk-je (both South Korea) on July 6, 2011.

LARGEST COLLECTION OF AUTOGRAPHED DRUMSTICKS

Peter Lavinger of New York has been collecting drumsticks ever since he caught one at a Good Rats gig in 1980. He has since amassed more than 1,300, all signed by various drumming rock stars from famous groups including The Beatles, Nirvana, and Pearl Jam.

4 YEARS 10 MONTHS 15 DAYS

Age of the **youngest professional drummer**, Julian Pavone (USA), when he played his 20th concert on March 29, 2009.

LONGEST DRUMMING MARATHON (INDIVIDUAL)

Playing at the Fórum de Castelo Branco shopping mall in Portugal from November 9 to 15, 2014, Portuguese musician Carlos Santos played his drums for an arm-numbing 133 hours 3 minutes straight. This beat the previous solo "drumathon" by more than 10 hours!

GUITAR HEROES

ARE YOU READY TO ROCK?

MOST AIR GUITAR CHAMPIONSHIPS WON

The annual Air Guitar World Championships is staged in Oulu, Finland. As of August 2015, three oxygen-strummers had won the title twice—Zac "The Magnet" Monro (UK, right) rocked to glory in 2001 and 2002, Ochi "Dainoji" Yosuke (Japan) won in 2006 and 2007, and France's Sylvian "Gunther Love" Guimene won in 2009 and 2010.

The **largest air guitar ensemble** (below) consisted of 2,377 "guitarists", organized by San Manuel Indian Bingo & Casino (USA) in Highland, California, on September 22, 2011.

LONGEST MARATHON PLAYING UKULELE

The ukulele is a small four-string instrument that resembles a miniature guitar and originates from Hawaii. On October 4–5, 2013, Glenn Haworth (Australia) played his ukulele for exactly 25 hours at the Haworth Music Store in Wollongong, New South Wales, Australia. In doing so, he raised an epic $10,000 for the Make-A-Wish Foundation charity.

MOST EXPENSIVE GUITAR SOLD AT AUCTION

This Fender Stratocaster raised a massive $2.7 million for charity when it was auctioned at the Ritz-Carlton hotel in Doha, Qatar, on November 17, 2005. The guitar had been signed by a host of famous rock stars, including Keith Richards of The Rolling Stones, Jimmy Page of Led Zeppelin, and Eric Clapton. Its sale totally annihilated the previous record of $959,500, which had been set by Eric Clapton's very own "Blackie" Fender Stratocaster on June 24, 2004.

SMALLEST GUITAR

Designed by scientists at New York's Cornell University in 1997, this Fender Strat wannabe measures just 10 micrometers long—that's one-twentieth the thickness of the average human hair! It was carved from silicon and its strings are 0.002 in (0.05 mm) thick. That's equivalent to 100 atoms laid end to end.

MOST VALUABLE GUITAR

If you missed out on buying the signed Stratocaster in Doha (see left), how about this Gibson SG? Designed by jewelry pioneer Aaron Shum, musician Mark Lui (both Hong Kong), and Gibson Guitars, the "Eden of Coronet" boasts 3.52 lb (1.6 kg) worth of gold, which has been embedded with sparkly Coronet diamonds. It was valued at a budget-busting $2 million on March 15, 2015.

7 MONTHS

Length of time it took to build this giant guitar. It was first used on June 6, 2000, with its players hitting the opening chord to "A Hard Day's Night" by The Beatles.

WOW!

LARGEST ELECTRIC GUITAR

Modeled on a 1967 Gibson Flying V, this 12:1-scale axe stands at 43 ft 7 in (13.29 m) in height and 16 ft 5 in (5.01 m) in width, and weighs in at 2,000 lb (900 kg). It was completed in 2000 by Scott Rippetoe (USA, above) and students from the Conroe Independent School District Academy of Science & Technology in Texas. Just imagine lugging it to band practice!

CHALLENGE

LET OUT YOUR INNER ROCK STAR!

6

Buttons on the new *Guitar Hero* controller, up from the original five. The strum bar and the whammy remain the same.

Do you harbor secret ambitions to one day be a rock star? With the release of *Guitar Hero Live* in 2015, with its first-person perspective, there's never been a better chance to experience what it feels like in front of a crowd at a concert.

The best thing about this challenge is that you can tailor the world record to your own tastes. Pick a song, practice to your heart's content, and then submit an application with your highest score for assessment. All variations will be considered, no matter the difficulty setting, the platform, or the number of players. Plus, it's not all about the new *Guitar Hero*. Feel free to dust off older editions and raise your top scores to record-breaking heights. Just be sure to supply all the settings when you apply!

HOW TO ATTEMPT A GUITAR HERO RECORD

1. SELECT HARDWARE
Choose which console you will be using and your favorite *Guitar Hero* game; it doesn't have to be the new *Guitar Hero Live*.

3. SOLO OR GROUP?
Decide if you'd rather do this as part of a team or would prefer to go for glory alone.

2. CHOOSE YOUR SONG
Make sure it's a tune that you like because you're going to be playing it a lot!

4. SET THE DIFFICULTY
Options range from Beginner to Expert. Bear in mind that the higher difficulty levels will have less competition.

5. PRACTICE
Get to know your song inside-out until you're confident your score is record-worthy. If it's not working, try a different one.

6. GO FOR IT!
Make sure you document all the settings and that the camera recording your attempt shows both you and the screen clearly. Now you're ready to rock!

THE RULES

Think you're ready to try for a record on *Guitar Hero*? For full guidelines and to apply, head to **www.guinnessworldrecords.com/blockbusters**, tell us the record you'd like to set, and submit your evidence! Here are a few general rules that apply to all GWR video-game record titles.

1. Video games records may only be attempted on a PC, an unmodified version of a commercially available games console, or an unmodified arcade cabinet/board. Alterations to hardware and/or software outside of those released or endorsed by the manufacturer will result in disqualification.

2. Records may be attempted only on platforms or systems for which the game in question has been commercially released.

3. No cheat codes or devices may be used at any point, unless specifically stated. Glitches may be used but must be preapproved by Guinness World Records.

4. Evidence must be submitted, including video evidence of the entire attempt as one continuous shot, encompassing the venue and the playthrough from power-on to final result.

OUT-OF-THIS-WORLD MUSIC

THE MUSIC INDUSTRY'S SHOOTING STARS

WOW!

FIRST MUSIC VIDEO FILMED IN SPACE

Canadian astronaut Commander Chris Hadfield took his music to new heights in 2013 when he performed a modified version of David Bowie's "Space Oddity" while on board the *International Space Station* (*ISS*; see box opposite). The high-altitude music video was a huge hit back on Earth, and Hadfield amassed some 770,000 Twitter followers during his time on the *ISS*— including a tweet from Bowie himself. As of August 7, 2015, the video had been watched 26,141,775 times on YouTube.

LARGEST SPACE STATION

The *International Space Station* is a record holder in its own right. Built piece by piece by a global collaboration of space agencies between 1998 and 2011, the station now orbits Earth at an average altitude of 248 miles (400 km), circling our planet every 90 minutes. End to end, the *ISS* measures just over 357 ft (109 m) long and weighs in at 924,739 lb (419,455 kg). The internal pressurized volume is 32,333 cu ft (916 m³)—about the same as a Boeing 747—though less than half of this is habitable.

FIRST LIVE MUSIC CONCERT BROADCAST TO SPACE

Paul McCartney (UK) may have set many records with legendary pop group The Beatles, but that's not stopping him from pushing new boundaries. In 2005, he transmitted a unique wake-up call to two astronauts on the *ISS*, from a concert he was performing in Anaheim, California. He serenaded them with two songs: "English Tea" and "Good Day Sunshine."

MUSIC

FESTIVAL FEVER

THE MUSIC INDUSTRY'S BEATING HEART

LONGEST-RUNNING POP MUSIC FESTIVAL

The UK's Reading Festival started out as the nomadic National Jazz (& Blues) Festival before moving to its permanent home in 1971. The three-day event has been held since 1961, making it the oldest annual popular music festival still in existence (pictured are attendees from 2014 and, inset, from 1975). It has hosted legendary acts such as Pink Floyd (1969), Nirvana (1992), and Eminem (2013). Metallica, Mumford & Sons, and The Libertines were 2015's headliners.

HIGHEST-GROSSING FESTIVAL

Over the weekends of April 10–12 and 17–19, 2015, the Coachella Valley Music and Arts Festival in Indio, California, grossed $84,264,264 from 198,000 ticket sales. As well as enjoying big acts such as Drake, Jack White, and Florence + The Machine, festival-goers were also dazzled by giant bugs (above).

LARGEST DISCO BALL

Little says glitz and glamour more than a disco ball, so you can only assume that 2014's Bestival, held on the Isle of Wight, UK, was truly a glitz-fest! The mega mirror ball, with a diameter of 33 ft 10 in (10.33 m), was made by British studio Newsubstance, who said of its construction: "It's taken three months of blood, sweat, and mirror tiles to design and fabricate this gigantic beast."

WOW!

MOST BODIES PAINTED

If you can't get messy at a music festival, then where can you? On July 31, 2015, it seems that 497 people at the Polish Woodstock Festival, aka Przystanek Woodstock, were inclined to agree, covering themselves in body paint to take the title with flying colors.

It's not the first time that the festival has celebrated a record. At the 2013 event, Polish telecoms network PLAY organized the **most people playing the same drum** (below). A total of 263 drummers were mustered to bash the 32-ft 10-in-wide (10-m) instrument. What did they play? Queen's "We Will Rock You," of course!

26

The **most music festivals visited in 30 days**, achieved by Greg Parmley (UK) in 2011. Countries on his epic tour included Belgium, Germany, Italy, Poland, Serbia, Switzerland, and the UK.

LONGEST MARATHON ON A DANCE GAME

Dance and fitness enthusiast Carrie Swidecki (USA) played *Just Dance 2014* for 76 hours 4 minutes 52 seconds in Bakersfield, California, from July 11 to 14, 2014. Carrie's record-breaking passion for the benefits of dance games can be infectious: "Exergaming encompasses everything I love in this world: dancing, sports, music, graphics, gaming, and education."

YOUNGEST GAMER TO SET A PERFECT SCORE ON *DANCE DANCE REVOLUTION*

Ryota Wada (Japan) has been playing *DDR* since he was just five. At the age of 9 years 288 days, he achieved a perfect "AAA" rating on the game, dancing to "Hyper Eurobeat" on the "Expert" difficulty setting at home in Tokyo on August 29, 2010. Sure-footed Ryota says that all it took for him to reach his perfect score was a nonslip surface!

FASTEST 20-METER MOONWALK

Accompanied by a selection of London's West End cast of *Thriller Live*—the stage show celebrating the music of the Jackson family—Michael Jackson fan and impersonator Ashiq Baluch (UK) moonwalked 20 m (65 ft 7 in) in just 6.53 seconds. The backward-gliding dancer set his record at London's Riverside Walkway on October 17, 2013. Will anyone else be able to *beat it*?

WOW!

MOST PROLIFIC DANCING GAME HIGH SCORER

Ranked No. 1 on the leaderboard of some 85 songs, Elizabeth "Kitty McScratch" Bolinger (USA) holds more high-score records for *Dance Central*, *Just Dance*, and *JD 2* than any other gamer. Her highest score was on *Dance Central*'s "C'mon N' Ride It (The Train)" by Quad City DJ's, for which she scored 432,793 points on December 5, 2010.

MOST BREAK-DANCE WINDMILLS IN 30 SECONDS

Try this without getting in a spin ... Mauro Peruzzi (Italy), also known as "Cico," performed a dizzying total of 50 windmills in only half a minute at the world finals of the Sony Ericsson UK B-Boy Championships in London, UK, on October 10, 2010. Mauro now offers break-dance tutorials online.

52.13 MILLION

Sales of Ubisoft's *Just Dance*, the **best-selling dance video-game series**, according to VGChartz. Nearest rival *Dance Dance Revolution* has sold "only" 21.59 million.

SING STARS

SUPERSINGERS HITTING THE HIGH NOTES

LONGEST KARAOKE MARATHON

Outsinging the previous record by almost 54 hours, Leonardo Polverelli (Italy, above) crooned for 101 hours 59 minutes 15 seconds on September 19–23, 2011, belting out 1,295 songs.

The **longest group karaoke marathon**, meanwhile, lasted 792 hours 2 minutes—that's 33 days!—in an event set up by Guangqi Honda Automobile Co., Ltd. (China), running from May 22 to June 24, 2014.

MOST "RATED" *SINGSTAR* COMMUNITY VIDEO

A homemade video of *SingStar* player "The_New_Guy" performing Tina Turner's "What's Love Got to Do with It?" is the most liked video on the *SingStar* community website. As of July 24, 2015, the video had received 28,014 heart "ratings," and 59,235 views since 2008. *SingStar* is the **best-selling karaoke video-game series**, with 21.81 million sales across all its titles.

LONGEST CAREER AS AN ELVIS IMPERSONATOR

Between 1955 and 2002, Victor Beasley from Belgium donned the famous white suit, curled his lip, and performed classics, such as "Jailhouse Rock," "Blue Suede Shoes," and "Love Me Tender." With 48 years impersonating Elvis Presley under his rhinestone-covered belt, Beasley has even been made an honorary citizen of Tupelo, Mississippi—birthplace of the "King" of rock 'n' roll.

17

Total number of Elvis Presley (USA) songs to hit the top spot on the US chart—the **most No. 1 singles by a male solo artist**. He is just beaten by Mariah Carey (USA) on 18, the **most US No. 1s by a solo artist**.

LARGEST GROUP OF CAROL SINGERS

Organized by the Godswill Akpabio Unity Choir of Nigeria, a festive army of 25,272 carol singers descended on the Uyo Township Stadium in Akwa Ibom, Nigeria, on December 13, 2014. The choir sang a medley of carols, including "The First Noël," "Joy to the World," and "O Come All Ye Faithful."

LONGEST TIME TO SING SUSPENDED UPSIDE DOWN

For some of us, the thought of singing on a stage is terrifying enough, but how about while hanging from the ceiling? Sourobhee Debbarma from India did just that on the set of *Guinness World Records— Ab India Todega* in 2011, performing for 4 minutes 35.39 seconds. What a headrush that must have been!

WOW!

MOST LIVE CONCERTS IN 24 HOURS (MULTIPLE CITIES)

You often hear pop stars grumbling about grueling tour schedules, but not country singer Hunter Hayes (USA). On May 9–10, 2014, he performed in 10 cities across six states in just one day, starting in New York, before traveling on to Boston, Worcester, Providence, New London, New Haven, Stamford (pictured), South Orange, Asbury Park, and finally Philadelphia. Hayes still found the energy to smile as he received his well-earned GWR certificate at the end of his gig marathon.

TOP 10
HIGHEST-EARNING MUSICIANS

1 KATY PERRY
$135 million

Katheryn Elizabeth "Katy" Hudson, aka Katy Perry (USA), has been breaking records since her 2008 debut hits "I Kissed a Girl" and "Hot n Cold" (see pp. 104–5). Her recent *Prismatic World Tour* encompassed 151 shows—85 of which were overseas—and was the highest-grossing tour in the USA by a female artist in 2014. In just two months, her concerts grossed $31 million from 21 performances in North America alone!

Perry's talents are not confined to the stage. She has also launched her own perfume range and founded her own record label—Metamorphosis. She even voiced Smurfette in 2011's hit movie *The Smurfs*!

2 GARTH BROOKS
$90 million

The US country music megastar came out of semi-retirement in September 2014 for a comeback tour, and earned up to $1 million per venue! Brooks—holder of the record for the **most Entertainer of the Year awards at the Academy of Country Music Awards**, with six wins—also found time to launch his own online music store, GhostTunes.

3 TAYLOR SWIFT
$80 million

4 CALVIN HARRIS
$66 million

With *1989*, her fifth studio album, country girl Taylor Swift (USA) continued her reinvention as a pop star. The album went platinum and its first single, "Shake It Off," went to no. 1 on the Billboard Hot 100. Like Katy Perry, she also has her own range of fragrances, and has begun to dabble with acting. She's also a noted philanthropist, with an interest in encouraging children to read.

Just behind Taylor in the earnings chart is boyfriend Calvin Harris (UK)— the DJ from Scotland who's become a global sensation. His fourth album, *Motion*, was released in 2014, and his image was plastered across billboards everywhere when he became the "face" of Giorgio Armani's underwear line. Together, Swift and Harris were named by Forbes as the **highest-earning celebrity couple**, taking over from Beyoncé and Jay Z (see right) with combined earnings in 2014–15 of $146 million!

5 JUSTIN TIMBERLAKE
$63.5 million

Rarely out of the highest-earners' chart is the former *NSYNC star, who returned to touring as a solo artist after a four-year break to pursue acting. His fourth studio album, *The 20/20 Experience—2 of 2*, debuted at No. 1 on the Billboard 200 in 2013, and gave Timberlake (USA) his highest-grossing tour.

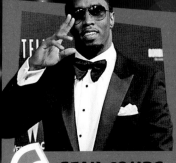

6 SEAN COMBS
$60 million

Although most famous as a performer, the majority of Diddy's (USA) earnings in 2014–15 came from business deals: for his own brand of vodka, his clothing and fragrance brands, and his stake in the Revolt film and TV network. But he also acts. *And* he's working on a new album, entitled—appropriately enough—*Money Making Mitch*.

7 LADY GAGA
$59 million

Tours, fragrances, acting, celebrity endorsements … it's been another great year for the woman otherwise known as Stefani Joanne Angelina Germanotta (USA). She may have hung up her meat dress, but "Mother Monster" continues to make an impact wherever she goes. She's even had an extinct wasp named after her!

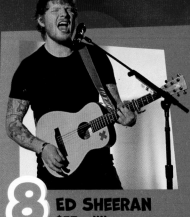

8 ED SHEERAN
$57 million

No one in the list of Top 10 highest-earning musicians gigged harder than Ed Sheeran (UK)—the English singer-songwriter played 154 concerts in the 12-month period analyzed by the money experts at *Forbes* magazine. Ed also benefited from a record-breaking 860 million streams on Spotify in 2014—the **most streams on Spotify in a year**.

9 JAY Z
$56 million

10 BEYONCÉ KNOWLES
$54.5 million

The second power couple in this year's chart is Mr. and Mrs. Carter (both USA), who together grossed more than $100 million with their 22-show stadium tour, *On the Run*.

When he's not rapping, multiple Grammy winner Jay Z—aka Shawn Corey Carter—is an entrepreneur with fingers in many pies, including real estate, video games, beverages, software fashion, and the Tidal music-streaming service.

Mrs. Carter—Beyoncé Knowles—last year occupied the top slot in the earnings chart but this year drops to 10th, bringing home a "mere" $54.5 million! This came from her tours and music sales, and also from endorsements and fronting her own fashion and sportswear brands.

Source: Forbes; earnings for the year ending June 2015

TV

SPONGEBOB SQUAREPANTS

RECORD-BREAKING IN BIKINI BOTTOM

WOW!

FIRST SPECIES NAMED AFTER A CHARACTER FROM *SPONGEBOB SQUAREPANTS*

A new species of lifeform found in Malaysia in 2010 looked so much like SpongeBob SquarePants that the biologist who found it named it *Spongiforma squarepantsii*. Despite the name, this new discovery is not a sponge—it's a fungus. What an honor for SpongeBob!

LARGEST CRAB

Mr. Krabs—aka Eugene Harold "Armor Abs" Krabs—might be a big shot in Bikini Bottom, but he's tiny compared with the world's biggest crabs. Japanese spider crabs (*Macrocheira kaempferi*), found off the coast of Japan, have legs up to 12 ft 1.5 in (3.69 m) long. Pictured left is "Big Daddy," from Sea Life in Blackpool, UK. His leg-span of 10 ft 2.5 in (3.11 m) makes him the **widest crustacean in captivity**.

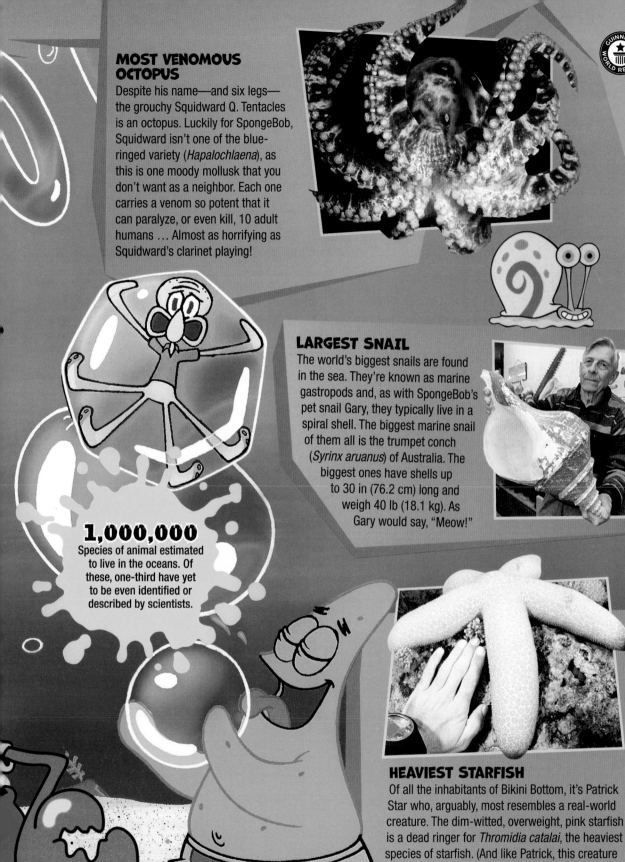

MOST VENOMOUS OCTOPUS

Despite his name—and six legs—the grouchy Squidward Q. Tentacles is an octopus. Luckily for SpongeBob, Squidward isn't one of the blue-ringed variety (*Hapalochlaena*), as this is one moody mollusk that you don't want as a neighbor. Each one carries a venom so potent that it can paralyze, or even kill, 10 adult humans … Almost as horrifying as Squidward's clarinet playing!

LARGEST SNAIL

The world's biggest snails are found in the sea. They're known as marine gastropods and, as with SpongeBob's pet snail Gary, they typically live in a spiral shell. The biggest marine snail of them all is the trumpet conch (*Syrinx aruanus*) of Australia. The biggest ones have shells up to 30 in (76.2 cm) long and weigh 40 lb (18.1 kg). As Gary would say, "Meow!"

1,000,000
Species of animal estimated to live in the oceans. Of these, one-third have yet to be even identified or described by scientists.

HEAVIEST STARFISH

Of all the inhabitants of Bikini Bottom, it's Patrick Star who, arguably, most resembles a real-world creature. The dim-witted, overweight, pink starfish is a dead ringer for *Thromidia catalai*, the heaviest species of starfish. (And like Patrick, this creature has no brain!) The biggest known specimen weighed 13 lb 3 oz (6 kg) … presumably *without* the Bermuda shorts!

CHALLENGE

SPONGEBOB'S COMING AT YOU!

MOST WET SPONGES THROWN AT A FACE IN ONE MINUTE

Inspired by Bikini Bottom's most famous resident, this sponge-themed record comes with a warning: you're going to get wet!

This is a two-person job, so once you've found a buddy, you'll have to decide who will be doing the throwing and who will be taking this challenge *face-on*. The record to beat is 43, so you'll probably want to do some practice throws. As SpongeBob might say: "I've just thought of something even funnier than 43 … 44!"

3:28:26
Marathon time ran by Larissa Tichon (Australia) wearing a SpongeBob costume in 2010—the **fastest marathon dressed as a cartoon character (female)**.

THE RULES

For the full guidelines and to apply, head to **www.guinnessworldrecords.com/blockbusters**.

1. The person attempting the record must throw the sponges from a distance of at least 10 ft (3 m) into the face of the second participant.

2. Commercially available sponges must be used; no sponge should exceed 10 x 6 in (25 x 15 cm) in size.

3. The 10-ft distance should be premeasured with two lines drawn for the thrower and receiver. The two participants must not step over their respective lines.

4. Next to the start line, the thrower must have a container of water. Before each throw, they must completely immerse the sponge in the water.

5. The thrower may have his/her hand in the container of water ready to throw the first sponge when the attempt starts.

6. Only sponges that hit the target full in the face are counted toward the final total. Two independent witnesses must decide if the sponges have achieved this, e.g. hitting the top of the head is not acceptable. The entire attempt must also be filmed for assessment.

7. One witness should be a professional timekeeper (e.g. from a local sports club) and should give clear start/finish signals to initiate and end the one-minute period.

THE RECORD TO BEAT

Regular record-setting duo Bipin Larkin and Ashrita Furman (both USA, Furman pictured) are the current holders of this wet 'n' wild title. On April 3, 2010, Bipin threw 43 sponges on target—Ashrita's face—in a minute. This bettered their own record of 29 sponges, achieved in 2009.

TOP TRIVIA

 As of 2015, *SpongeBob SquarePants* has earned the **most Nickelodeon Kids' Choice Awards for a cartoon**: 12.

There have been two SpongeBob feature films to date—one in 2004 and a sequel in 2015. Between them, they have grossed $543,645,287 worldwide.

The creator of *SpongeBob SquarePants*, Stephen Hillenburg (USA), is formerly a teacher of marine biology, so he has plenty of expertise to draw on!

TEENAGE MUTANT NINJA TURTLES

HEROES IN A HALF SHELL

DID YOU KNOW?

Although they are best known as TV and movie stars, the pizza-loving Ninja Turtles started life in a comic book created by Kevin Eastman (left) and Peter Laird (both USA). They named their four lead turtles—Leonardo, Michelangelo, Raphael, and Donatello—after Italian Renaissance artists.

LARGEST TURTLE

In scientific terms, the TMNTs are red-eared sliders (*Trachemys scripta elegans*)—the most popular species of turtle kept as a pet in the USA. These turtles average 6–8 in (15–20 cm) long, so they are quite a lot smaller than the leatherback turtle (*Dermochelys coriacea*), the largest living species, which can reach 7 ft (2.1 m) in length!

LARGEST PIZZA COMMERCIALLY AVAILABLE

The Ninja Turtles were famous for their wacky taste in pizza—taste combos such as tuna fish and peanut butter, or butterscotch and anchovies—so they might find this plentiful pepperoni pizza a little bland. But they wouldn't leave hungry! The "Giant Sicilian" at Big Mama's & Papa's Pizzeria in Los Angeles is 20.25 sq ft (1.87 m²)—as big as the diner's booths! Just give them 24 hours' notice if you want to order it.

HIGHEST SCORE ON *TMNT: TURTLES IN TIME*

The remarkable reptiles received the video-game treatment in 1991 when they starred in the arcade game *Teenage Mutant Ninja Turtles: Turtles in Time*. Top of the high-score table is David Price (USA), who used a single credit to reach a turtle-y amazing score of 212 points at the New York Comic Con on February 7, 2009.

LARGEST GATHERING OF PEOPLE DRESSED AS NINJA TURTLES

Did you know that the collective noun for turtles is a "bale" or "turn" of turtles? We're not sure if this term applies to humans dressed as Ninja Turtles, but if it did, the largest bale would be 1,394 people, achieved by the Nickelodeon Suites Resort in Orlando, Florida, on August 9, 2014 (left). This is the second time that Nickelodeon Suites have broken the record—the main picture shows their 836-strong effort at the Mall of America in Bloomington, Minnesota, the year before.

WOW!

TV SCOOBY-DOO

PUTTING THE "GREAT" INTO GREAT DANE!

LARGEST COLLECTION OF SCOOBY-DOO MEMORABILIA

Rebecca Findlay of West Vancouver, Canada, has to be the world's biggest Scooby-Doo fan. And there's no mystery why—her home is littered with a record-breaking 1,116 unique items of Scoob-related merchandise. She's been collecting since the age of 17, and owns everything from posters and bedclothes to a pinball machine and even a Scooby-Doo tattoo!

TALLEST DOG

Zoinks! It's Zeus, the closest thing to a real-life Scooby-Doo! Like Scooby, Zeus was a Great Dane—not just the tallest Great Dane, but also the tallest dog of any breed … ever! A much-loved member of the Doorlag family of Otsego in Michigan, Zeus measured a mammoth 3 ft 8 in (1.118 m) to the shoulder. Although he passed away in 2014, his record height has never been beaten.

MOST TENNIS BALLS IN A DOG'S MOUTH

Here's a dog that could compete with Scooby-Doo for having the largest mouth … but instead of cramming his face with Scooby snacks, Augie the doggie here prefers tennis balls! The gifted golden retriever managed to fit five normal-size tennis balls between his jaws at the family home in Dallas, Texas. New balls, please!

324 EPISODES

of Scooby-Doo have been made, across 24 seasons and 11 different series, from *Scooby-Doo, Where Are You!* on September 13, 1969, to *Scooby-Doo! Mystery Incorporated*, on April 5, 2013.

OLDEST GHOST

Ghost Ranch, in north-central New Mexico's Rio Arriba County, sounds like the perfect setting for a Scooby-Doo mystery … and indeed it's reportedly haunted by the ghostly spirit of a prehistoric phytosaur. Its skeleton was found in 1949, and since then people have reported seeing a 20-ft-long (6-m) snakelike apparition. At 220 million years old, this would make the phytosaur the oldest ghost!

DID YOU KNOW?

Scooby-Doo, Where Are You! was a TV show created by Joe Ruby and Ken Spears in 1969. It introduced the world to Scoobert "Scooby" Doo—the Great Dane best friend of the amateur sleuth Norville "Shaggy" Rogers and the Mystery Inc. gang (Fred, Daphne, and Velma). Scooby and the crew have appeared in numerous TV series and two Hollywood movies (below, left). A new TV series, *Be Cool, Scooby-Doo!*, is due to air on Boomerang in late 2015.

CHALLENGE

GET READY, IT'S MORPHIN' TIME!

LARGEST COLLECTION OF POWER RANGERS MEMORABILIA

Calling all Power Rangers fans! If your room is jam-packed with all things Power Rangers, you could be a contender for this record. It doesn't matter what the items are—whether your passion is action figures, posters, video games, books, DVDs, costumes, T-shirts, pajamas, or indeed all of them, as long as it's official Power Rangers merchandise, it counts. *Go Go,* collectors!

22 SEASONS in the *Power Rangers* TV franchise across 19 series, as of 2015. The latest to air is Saban's *Power Rangers Dino Charge* on Nickelodeon.

THE RULES

For the full guidelines and to apply, head to **www.guinnessworldrecords.com/blockbusters**.

1. This record is based on the total number of *different* individual items in the collection. Duplicates do not count. If items are usually paired, e.g. earrings or cuff links, the number of matching pairs should be given.

2. A concise and audited inventory must be submitted in the form of a spreadsheet or log book. The total number of items in the collection must be clearly stated here and countersigned by two witnesses. One of the signed statements of authentication must come from a relevant recognized society specializing in toy memorabilia.

3. Applicants must provide a brief history of when (year) and why the collection began—feel free to also tell us where you store the items and if you have a particular favorite!

TOP TRIVIA

Red and Blue are the only two colors to appear in every Power Rangers team to date.

Former Green Power Ranger Jason David Frank (USA) is also a former record holder. In 2010, he achieved the **most pine boards broken during freefall**: seven. The current total stands at 12.

The villain in the first *Mighty Morphin Power Rangers* movie, released in 1995, was called Ivan Ooze.

CHIPMUNKS, FLINTSTONES & MICKEY MOUSE

BEST-SELLING ANIMATED CARTOON BAND

The squeaky-voice trio of Alvin & The Chipmunks started out singing novelty Christmas songs and quickly became the stars of their own comics, TV shows, and movies. Since their debut in 1958, they have sold an estimated 50 million albums!

LARGEST GATHERING OF PEOPLE DRESSED AS CARTOON CHARACTERS

County Monaghan in Ireland returned to the Stone Age in July 2010 for a gathering of *Flintstones* fans. In all, 905 people dressed as Fred, Wilma, Barney, and Betty … and someone even brought along their dog dressed as Dino the pet dinosaur.

LARGEST COLLECTION OF MICKEY MOUSE MEMORABILIA

Mickey mania has definitely gripped Janet Esteves of Katy in Texas. For more than 40 years, she has collected every conceivable piece of Mickey Mouse memorabilia, and currently owns 8,170 unique items. Mouse-mad Janet fell in love with Mickey in the 1970s during her honeymoon in Disneyland.

WOW!

FIRST FICTIONAL CHARACTER HONORED ON THE WALK OF FAME

On November 13, 1978, Disney's iconic star Mickey Mouse became the first fictional character on the Hollywood Walk of Fame. The star-lined street—stretching for 1.7 mi (2.7 km) along 15 blocks—celebrates more than 2,550 of the world's most famous media superstars.

MICKEY MOUSE

SESAME STREET

ST

NO STRINGS ATTACHED

150 COUNTRIES

The range of the Sesame Workshop, the educational organization behind the TV show. It has been advocating numeracy and literacy everywhere from Australia to Yemen since 1968.

LARGEST COLLECTION OF SESAME STREET MEMORABILIA

Even Count von Count (right) might struggle adding up all the items owned by *Sesame Street* superfan Sheila Chustek (USA). As of June 18, 2014, her collection stood at 942. Can you guess which character is her favorite?

MOST COOKIES BAKED IN ONE HOUR

The Cookie Monster would probably be more interested in a record for **most cookies *eaten* in one hour**, but for Hassett's Bakery in Cork, Ireland, it was all about the baking. As part of the annual Irish Redhead Convention on July 30, 2013, the bakery produced a staggering 4,695 cookies. Did Elmo, the furry red monster (right) attend?

BIG BIRDS: THE RIVALS

He's one of *Sesame Street*'s most iconic characters, and at 8 ft 2 in (2.49 m) he's pretty hard to miss. But how does Big Bird size up to real-life avian giants? Well, the ostrich, the **largest living bird**, just beats him at 9 ft (2.74 m) tall. However, the **largest bird ever** would have towered over them both; the elephant bird of Madagascar, which became extinct around 1,000 years ago, reached up to 11 ft (3.3 m)!

11 FT

9 FT

8 FT 2 IN

MOST COMPLETE WOOLLY MAMMOTH

In 2007, an ancient ancestor of Mr. Snuffleupagus, aka Snuffy (right), was unearthed in Russia. Christened Lyuba, the 110-lb (50-kg) female calf (above) is the most intact woolly mammoth (*Mammuthus primigenius*) ever discovered, with skin, internal organs, and even some fur. She is now on display at Shemanovskiy Museum in Salekhard, Russia.

WOW!

MOST EMMY AWARDS WON BY A TV SERIES

When it was conceived in 1968, *Sesame Street*'s combination of education and entertainment was something of a departure for children's TV. The experiment clearly paid off, however, according to the critics; as of 2015, the PBS show had received an epic 159 Emmys!

MOST EMMY AWARDS FOR AN ANIMATED SERIES

The Simpsons has been winning Emmy awards since 1990, when creator Matt Groening first picked up a trophy for the episode "Life on the Fast Lane." In total, the yellow family has been nominated for 78 Primetime Emmy awards in nine different categories and won a record 31 of them (in four categories). Let's hope there's room on the Simpson mantelpiece for all those trophies!

LARGEST COLLECTION OF *SIMPSONS* MEMORABILIA

Ay caramba! Cameron Gibbs of Skye in Victoria, Australia, had amassed 2,580 different items of *Simpsons* merchandise as of March 20, 2008. Every conceivable piece of memorabilia fills his bedroom from board games and action figures to posters and plush toys—Cameron's own version of the Springsonian Museum!

WOW!

LONGEST-RUNNING SITCOM (EPISODES)

The Simpsons first appeared in short segments on *The Tracey Ullman Show*, starting on April 19, 1987. It wasn't until December 17, 1989, that they got their own show … and they've not been off our screens since—a record-breaking 574 episodes across 26 years as of May 17, 2015, and counting!

33.6 MILLION

Audience for the most watched *Simpsons* episode, "Bart Gets an 'F'" (1990), according to the Internet Movie Database.

MOST TATTOOS FROM THE SAME ANIMATED TV SERIES

Michael Baxter has taken his love of *The Simpsons* to extremes ... by tattooing 203 different characters from the show all over his back! Michael—a prison officer from Bacchus Marsh in Victoria, Australia—spent 130 hours and around $12,000 on his skin-credible work of art.

AN INTERVIEW WITH: MATT GROENING

Simpsons creator Matt Groening based his comedy capers on his own family, and his own childhood provided the inspiration for Bart.

Do you still enjoy making the show?

It's so much fun, I love working on it. But that's not to take away from the incredibly diligent work of the brilliant animators and writers. This has been a collaborative effort from the beginning and I feel honored to be part of the team.

Do you have a favorite episode?

I like a lot of the very early episodes, particularly ones with Lisa. When Lisa first meets Bleeding Gums Murphy, her saxophone mentor, I was amazed that the show could actually be moving, given how garishly the characters were drawn.

And a favorite record?

The one I remember the most as a kid was Robert Earl Hughes, the world's fattest man [**largest chest measurement (male)**]. When he died, he had to be buried in a piano case—and that has stuck with me for life ... scarred me for life! We did an episode in which Homer had gained a huge amount of weight and was buried in a piano case ... and the cable broke! It's fun when we can do this type of thing!

MORE SIMPSONS THIS WAY!

MATT GROENING

TV THE SIMPSONS

REAL-WORLD SPRINGFIELD

TALLEST DOUGHNUT STACK

D-oh try this at home, Homer! All you need to beat the record held by UK staff at 20th Century Fox and Capital Radio is a couple of thousand ring doughnuts and the ability to stack them as high as you can— at least 3 ft 7.5 in (110.5 cm) to be sure of success.

WOW!

LARGEST PLAYABLE SAXOPHONE

Lisa's pretty good on the saxophone, but she'd probably struggle staying upright with this one, let alone playing a tune on it! The custom-made instrument stands at a staggering 8 ft 11 in (2.74 m) tall, with a bell diameter of 1 ft 3.3 in (39.1 cm). It was created by J'Elle Stainer (Brazil) in 2013.

144

LARGEST COLLECTION OF PACIFIERS

You might think that the youngest Simpson's devotion to pacifiers is impossible to beat, but Dr. Muhammad Mustansar from Pakistan easily exceeds Maggie in terms of quantity, with 1,994 to his name. However, his motive for collecting isn't his penchant for pacifiers—he actually gathers them as a way of *deterring* people from using them!

TALLEST HAIRSTYLE

If you thought that Marge's hairdo was sky-high, wait until you hear about this … Using a combination of real and fake tresses, a group of hairdressers constructed a coiffure that towered a hair-raising 8 ft 8.76 in (2.66 m) tall at an event organized by hair salon chain KLIPP unser Frisör in Wels, Austria, on June 21, 2009.

13

Number of cities named Springfield in the USA. It was long-debated which was the namesake of the Simpsons' hometown, and in 2012 creator Matt Groening confirmed that it was the Springfield in Oregon.

FASTEST SKATEBOARD SPEED (STANDING)

If Bart were able to reach speeds like this, he'd never have to worry about being caught by Homer, Principal Skinner, or anyone else for that matter. Canadian pro boarder Mischo Erban hit a blistering 80.74 mph (129.94 km/h) at Les Éboulements in Quebec, Canada, on June 18, 2012. Ay caramba!

TV DOCTOR WHO

"WHO ARE YOU? I AM THE DOCTOR!"

LARGEST COLLECTION OF DOCTOR WHO MEMORABILIA

Doctor Who fans are known as "Whovians," and who could be more of a Whovian than Ian O'Brien of Manchester, UK? Since 1974, Ian has been collecting *Doctor Who* action figures, models, books, posters, DVDs, and, in fact, anything related to the Time Lord and his foes. As of July 25, 2015, he owned a time-warping 2,021 items. We guess that this makes Ian an *Item* Lord, rather than a Time Lord!

MOST EXPENSIVE DALEK

Here's one item that Whovian collector Ian (see left) would love to have in his collection—a full-size blue "Dalek Supreme" first seen on TV in the 1970s. He'd need a *TARDIS*-like piggy bank if he wanted to buy it, though—the last time it went on sale, in 2005, it sold for a record-breaking $61,934 … even though it had been blown up on TV and then patched back together again!

LARGEST COLLECTION OF DALEKS

Someone else undoubtedly eager to get their hands on the Dalek Supreme above is Dalek collector Rob Hull from Doncaster in the UK. His home is swarming with a record-breaking 1,801 Daleks of varying sizes, ranging from tiny figurines to a radio-controlled full-size prop that even issues the Skaro mutants' terrifying war cry: "Exterminate!"

WOW!

LONGEST-RUNNING SCIENCE FICTION TV SERIES

As of Christmas Day 2014, a total of 813 episodes of *Doctor Who* (BBC, UK) had been aired. This total includes a full-length TV movie but does not include spoofs, spin-offs, or webisodes. The latest (12th) incarnation of the Doctor is played by Peter Capaldi (left), assisted by companion Clara Oswald (Jenna Coleman, right).

LARGEST DALEK

Snugburys Ice Cream (UK) have been making straw sculptures for more than 10 years and, in 2013, constructed a 35-ft-tall (10.6-m) sculpture of a Dalek. The "*strawe*some" creation, made in celebration of *Doctor Who*'s 50th anniversary, took 700 hours to complete and used 13,000 lb (6 metric tonnes) of straw and 11,000 lb (5 metric tonnes) of steel.

1 THE SIMPSONS
574 episodes

Everyone's favorite dysfunctional family from Springfield has been entertaining us for more than 25 years. It is currently on Season 26, as of July 2015, and the next two seasons of the animated sitcom are already commissioned. Its self-titled feature film—guest-starring Tom Hanks, Joe Mantegna, and rock band Green Day—was a huge hit, earning $527,071,022 in 2007.

2 THE BUGS BUNNY & TWEETY SHOW
387 episodes

TV's most famous wisecracking "wabbit" actually started out on the big screen, introduced in a *Merrie Melodies* short film in 1940. His small-screen debut came in 1960, and he has maintained a regular presence ever since. Along with fellow Looney Tunes star Tweety, his longest series ran from 1986 to 2000.

3 ARTHUR
215 episodes

If you thought that all aardvarks did was sleep and eat ants, you clearly haven't seen *Arthur*. Based on the books by Marc Brown, the series centers on eight-year-old aardvark Arthur Read and his friends, and is the longest-running animated series to air on PBS. Well regarded for its handling of sensitive issues, such as illnesses, the show has featured many guest stars, including Matt Damon and Joan Rivers.

4 TEENAGE MUTANT NINJA TURTLES
193 episodes

Inspired by a comic-book series, the TV debut of the heroes in a half shell is their most enduring (1987–96). In its wake followed a Japanese anime spin-off, a live-action series, and two more toons—the latest series of which is still running on Nickelodeon.

5 SPONGEBOB SQUAREPANTS
190 episodes

SpongeBob, Squidward, and Mr. Krabs, along with all the other residents of Bikini Bottom, first swam on to our screens back in 1999. The world's most optimistic sponge got his very own feature film in 2015—*Sponge Out of Water*—which earned a respectable $311,394,032 at the box office. Not bad for a guy who lives in a pineapple!

265 MILLION
Number of Bugs Bunny stamps printed in 1997. It was the first US postage stamp to feature a cartoon character. Mickey Mouse must have been pretty peeved!

= 6 **DORA THE EXPLORER**
172 episodes

Dora has been embarking on quests with monkey companion Boots since 2000. Although the original helped us to learn Spanish, there have now been 30-plus foreign adaptations, in which Dora speaks everything from Arabic and Hindi to Norwegian.

= 6 **RUGRATS**
172 episodes

Tied with Dora on 172, the Rugrats (1991–2004) were arguably the planet's most famous toddlers. It was once Nickelodeon's wonderkid, and became the channel's longest-running animated series. It also picked up the **most Kids' Choice "Favorite Cartoon" awards** (six; 1996–2001). But SpongeBob has since claimed both titles, with 12 awards, as of 2015.

All figures correct as of July 23, 2015

8 THE FLINTSTONES
166 episodes

TV's biggest Stone Age icons—originally called the Flagstones—first premiered in 1960 and ran for six years. The classic got a 2015 spin-off in the form of direct-to-DVD movie *The Flintstones and WWE: Stone Age SmackDown.* Yabba-dabba-KO!

9 THE FAIRLY ODDPARENTS
152 episodes

Teaching us to be careful what you wish for since 2001, Nickelodeon surely couldn't have wished for more success. The magical adventures of Timmy and his fairy godparents have even inspired three live-action films.

10 STAR WARS: THE CLONE WARS
121 episodes

It's not the first time that lightsabers and stormtroopers have received the cartoon treatment, but this Lucasfilm series lasted the longest (2008–14). Set in the same era as *Episode II*, it follows the battles of Obi-Wan, Anakin, and his apprentice, Ahsoka (pictured).

APPS & ONLINE

APPS

ANGRY BIRDS VS. CUTE KITTENS ...

FIRST APP TO BE WITHDRAWN AFTER TOPPING THE APPLE APP STORE CHART

Dong Nguyen of Vietnam sure knows how to make gaming history not once, but twice. First, the software developer made the incredibly addictive *Flappy Bird* back in April 2013. Then he became the first person to pull an app from sale due to it selling too well! On February 10, 2014, after *Flappy Bird* had flown to top of the Apple App Store charts in the USA, the UK, and China, Nguyen decided to stop selling it because he was worried that its addictiveness might be dangerous.

MOST VIEWED TRAILER FOR AN APP

If you ever needed proof that everyone loves a cute kitty, then here it is. As of August 27, 2015, the trailer for the *My Talking Tom* app had been viewed a mega 145,914,010 times on YouTube. The app centers on a kitten called Tom, who you nurture to adulthood. Meow!

CLASH of CLANS

MOST SUCCESSFUL *CLASH OF CLANS* PLAYER

Since its release in 2012, MMO strategy game *Clash of Clans* has had players vying for supremacy in a colorful, fantasy world. As of August 27, 2015, player "saad" of the 48-man clan "Arab Champions" was ranked the world's No. 1 player after facing fierce competition to emerge victorious with 4,986 trophies.

30 COUNTRIES

Number of nations represented by attendees at the first official *Clash of Clans* convention— ClashCon—held in Helsinki, Finland, in October 2015. These included Japan, the USA, India, and Australia.

MOST THEME PARKS BASED ON A VIDEO GAME

You've played the video game, now visit the theme park! As of August 2015, there were 11 official fun parks based on the feathery app stars. Two of them are located in the UK, and China, Malaysia, Russia, and Spain all have one. The rest can be found in Finland— home to *Angry Birds* creator Rovio—with the biggest located at the Särkänniemi adventure park (pictured).

FIRST MOVIE BASED ON A MOBILE APP

Already massive stars on mobile screens, the *Angry Birds* are readying their wings for big-screen domination. On May 15, 2013, Rovio entered into a marketing and distribution agreement with Sony Pictures Entertainment for *The Angry Birds Movie*, a feature-length animation based on the record-breaking app series. Starring a whole host of comic talent, it was set for release in May 2016. Look out for a cameo from YouTube megastars SMOSH.

FIRST MOBILE GAME SERIES TO REACH 1 BILLION DOWNLOADS

On May 9, 2012, Finnish games developer Rovio Entertainment announced that its *Angry Birds* games had been downloaded more than 1 billion times since debuting in December 2009. The series continues to soar higher than a catapulted eagle. *Angry Birds 2* flew from its roost on July 30, 2015, and was downloaded more than 40 million times in just three weeks.

WOW!

MORE APPS THIS WAY ...

APPS

TRAVEL, MUSIC, PIRATES & MORE!

WOW!

MOST TRACKED ARTIST ON SONGKICK

Songkick is the perfect app for music lovers who want to keep tabs on the whereabouts of their favorite artists, without having to trawl through the music press or poorly updated websites. It can even send you alerts when your top artists are playing locally. As of July 31, 2015, the most tracked act was UK rock group Coldplay (right), with 1,428,859 fans monitoring the band's every move.

FIRST APP FOR PIRACY

Yarrr, it's true, there really is an app for everything … ASAM (Anti-Shipping Activity Messages) serves one purpose: to keep people at sea safe by supplying the latest news about pirate attacks and hijackings around the world's oceans. One happy customer on iTunes put it succinctly: "I pretty much check this application before leaving the house every day. It's like traffic reports, except pirates."

FIRST ANDROID APP TO REACH 1 BILLION DOWNLOADS

It hasn't got many bells and whistles, but that hasn't detracted from Gmail's popularity. On May 14, 2014, Google announced that its iconic email application had surpassed the 1-billion milestone—that's almost one copy for every seven humans on Earth! Various app series have attained a billion downloads, but Gmail was the first single stand-alone app to achieve the feat.

MOST STREAMED TRACK ON SPOTIFY

Between August 28 and September 3, 2015, "What Do You Mean?" by Canadian musician Justin Bieber, was streamed 30,723,708 times on the online music streaming service, smashing the previous record held by One Direction's "Drag Me Down." The single debuted at No. 1 on the Billboard Hot 100 too, entering Bieber into a select group, which includes Taylor Swift's "Shake It Off" (2014), Katy Perry's "Part of Me" (2012), and Lady Gaga's "Born This Way" (2011).

FIRST APP GIVING ACCESS TO A COUNTRY'S ARCHEOLOGY

In 2013, the four archeological trusts of Wales, UK, joined forces to bring their nation's history bang into the 21st century. Archwilio, which means "to examine" or "to explore" in Welsh, is a tie-in to a more extensive website. The app allows users to view details and photos of Wales' most prestigious ancient landmarks, such as Neolithic burial site Pentre Ifan (above), as well as letting amateur historians add their own updates.

MOST REVIEWS POSTED ON TRIPADVISOR

For jet-setters forever on the go, an app is a much handier way of accessing one of the web's biggest travel portals. No other TripAdvisor contributor has written more articles than Hong Kong-based Brad Reynolds (USA), with 3,323 reviews under "BradJill" (Jill is his wife), as of February 2015. Above, he is pictured before India's Taj Mahal, and inset at the Vatican City in Italy in 2012—his highest-scoring review to date, having earned 254 points.

LARGEST INSTANT MESSAGING SERVICE ACQUISITION

Sending text messages is so last decade … Nowadays it's all about instant messaging apps—at least that's how Facebook seems to see it, as the social-networking giant forked out a record-breaking $16 billion to acquire WhatsApp in 2014. Along with similar messaging services, such as Snapchat and Facebook's own rival Messenger, WhatsApp frequently appears high in the free app charts.

KICKSTARTER

MOST MONEY PLEDGED ...

WOW!

ON A CROWDSOURCING PLATFORM

You can't talk about crowdsourcing without mentioning Kickstarter, so it's little wonder that the online platform—cofounded by Charles Adler, Perry Chen, and Yancey Strickler (all USA, left to right above)—attracts the most crowdfunders. As of August 5, 2015, some 9.1 million people had pledged $1,871,520,731, funding at least 90,154 projects. On the flipside, 14% never took a single pledge! Here, we celebrate some of Kickstarter's most successful projects to date.

funded with

KICK STARTER

FOR A MUSIC PROJECT

Kickstarter is the perfect platform to promote yourself. Amanda Palmer's (USA) "The new RECORD, ART BOOK, and TOUR" project received $1,192,793 by June 1, 2012. After her success, she not only released a new album in 2012—*Theatre is Evil*—but also a memoir, titled *The Art of Asking* ... As any Kickstarter aficionado will know, if you don't ask, you don't get.

FOR A FASHION PROJECT

The "10-year hoodie," made by Jake Bronstein (USA), is so robust that it will allegedly last for a lifetime. The designer even offers to repair any damage caused in its first 10 years. It beat its $50,000 goal on April 21, 2013, with $1,053,830 pledged by 9,226 backers.

FOR A 3D TECHNOLOGY PROJECT

3D printing has yet to hit the mainstream market in a big way, but engineering group M3D is looking to change that with its Micro 3D printer, which had earned $3,401,361 from 11,855 backers on Kickstarter, as of May 7, 2014. The colorful cube-shape printers are compact for homes—7.3 in (18.5 cm) per side—and currently retail for $349.

M3D

FOR A CHILDREN'S BOOK

Augie & The Green Knight, written by US author Zachary Weiner, is described as "an adventure story about a scientifically precocious young girl in a world of fantasy." By July 2, 2014, the project had received $384,410—as pledged by a total of 9,044 backers.

FOR A MOVIE

Fans of TV series *Veronica Mars*, which was canceled in 2007, rallied together to bring their favorite private investigator to the big screen. The appeal began on March 13, 2013, and amassed a total of $5,702,153. The eponymous movie premiered on March 14, 2014, just a year and a day after the appeal was launched.

FOR A COMIC

Rich Burlew's (USA) "*The Order of the Stick* Reprint Drive" was funded on February 21, 2012, to the tune of $1,254,120 by 14,952 backers. The author sought backing to reprint his *The Order of the Stick* books. The comics are typified by their colorful stick-man-style illustrations, though in later editions the characters have been "filled out" a bit (inset).

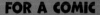

FOR A VIDEO GAME

After its surprise announcement at E3 2015, upcoming action-adventure title *Shenmue III* (Ys Net, Japan) raised $6,333,296 by July 17, 2015—smashing the previous record of $5,545,991. *Shenmue III* also achieved the **fastest $1 million pledged for a crowdfunded video game**, reaching that milestone in just 1 hour 44 minutes.

MINECRAFT
A BLOCKBUSTING SUCCESS STORY

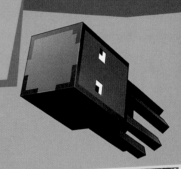

LARGEST LEGO MINECRAFT DIORAMA

Measuring 184 sq ft (17.13 m²) in area, this blockbusting sculpture was created with LEGO® Minecraft pieces at the Brick 2014 exhibition in London, UK, from November 27–30, 2014.

All attendees were given the chance to contribute to the diorama by building on a 16-stud-wide square board before they were assembled by LEGO Co-Creation Manager Julie Broberg and her team. The 3D scene made a fantasy cityscape.

BEST-SELLING iOS APP

As of February 2015, Minecraft: Pocket Edition—designed specifically for mobile devices—had sold more than 30 million copies. According to Apple, it secured the top spot as the best-selling paid app—not just game—of 2014 on both iPhone and iPad, despite having been released back in 2011.

Minecraft has quickly become the **best-selling game on home-computer formats**, shifting a total of 18.9 million units on PC/Mac, as of March 2015.

LONGEST MINECRAFT MARATHON

It's easy to lose track of time when you're constructing your way through Markus "Notch" Persson's blocky building game. One man who plays with his eye on the clock, however, is record-breaking Martin Fornleitner of Vienna, Austria. On August 19–20, 2011, Martin played Minecraft on a Sony Xperia Play handset for 24 hours 10 minutes. This equates to 72.5 in-game days of play. "I like the 'Adventure' mode," says Martin, "because it's fun to fight Creepers and search for resources."

7,767 MILES

Average distance between a player's spawn point and the fabled Far Lands in the preversion-1.8 release of *Minecraft*. Kurt (below) has covered just 16% of this distance.

FIRST LEGO SET FOR AN INDIE VIDEO GAME

The 480-piece LEGO *Minecraft* Micro World set launched in June 2012 for $34.99 in the USA. A group of three *Minecraft* fans submitted their design for the set on the LEGO CUUSOO site, which encourages new ideas for LEGO designs. After receiving the 10,000 public votes required, LEGO began manufacturing the set. One *Minecraft* block is represented as one 1x1 LEGO plate.

WOW!

LONGEST JOURNEY IN *MINECRAFT*

In March 2011, Kurt J. Mac (USA) began an epic journey to the edge of *Minecraft*'s vast world in "Survival" mode, recording his voyage on his YouTube channel. By April 10, 2015—four years into the trek—he had crossed 1,303 miles (2,097.1 km), or 2,097,152 blocks from his original spawn site.

KEEP ON DIGGING:
• **THERE'S MORE *MINECRAFT* TO COME**

159

MINECRAFT
BUILDING IT BIG IN THE OVERWORLD

LONGEST TRIP ON A ROLLER COASTER IN *MINECRAFT*

Building minecart tracks is a fun part of *Minecraft*, but some players have used the game's rail-building tools for even more extreme purposes—to create roller coasters! The ride made by Planet Minecraft user "Gaermine" of the Czech Republic is one epic example. Built in May 2013, the coaster is a sweeping, sky-reaching monstrosity that takes users 50 minutes to ride from start to end!

LARGEST *MINECRAFT* CATHEDRAL

It took *Minecraft* user "GNRfrancis" (UK) more than a year to build this epic cathedral called, appropriately enough, *Epic Cathedral*! It was uploaded on October 30, 2012, and its spires, buttresses, and stained-glass windows required an incredible 2,082,348 blocks. Pictured inset is a view of the intricately tiled nave, showing enhanced shading.

LARGEST *MINECRAFT* RESORT

Covering 43 sq mi (111 km²), Florida's Walt Disney World Resort is one of the largest entertainment complexes on the planet. As of February 3, 2015, the MCMagic server had re-created five of the resort's six theme and water parks. Every ride and show is present, and costumed "cast members" are on hand to help.

WOW!

4 MONTHS
Build time spent by "therealduckie" and a team of 25 creators to complete the basic Walt Disney World Resort in 1:1 scale in *Minecraft*.

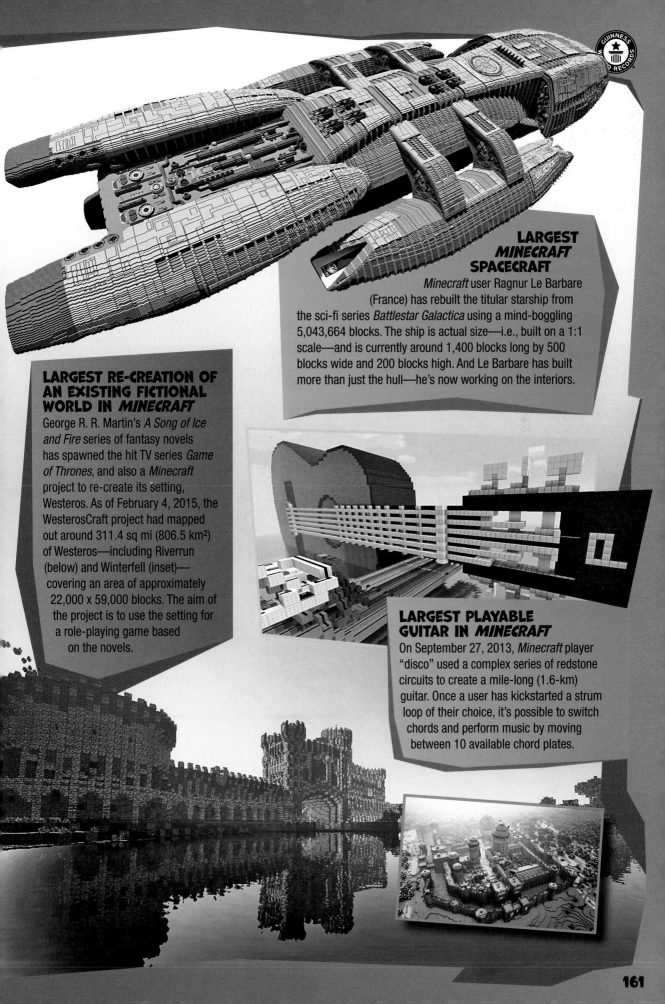

LARGEST MINECRAFT SPACECRAFT

Minecraft user Ragnur Le Barbare (France) has rebuilt the titular starship from the sci-fi series *Battlestar Galactica* using a mind-boggling 5,043,664 blocks. The ship is actual size—i.e., built on a 1:1 scale—and is currently around 1,400 blocks long by 500 blocks wide and 200 blocks high. And Le Barbare has built more than just the hull—he's now working on the interiors.

LARGEST RE-CREATION OF AN EXISTING FICTIONAL WORLD IN MINECRAFT

George R. R. Martin's *A Song of Ice and Fire* series of fantasy novels has spawned the hit TV series *Game of Thrones*, and also a *Minecraft* project to re-create its setting, Westeros. As of February 4, 2015, the WesterosCraft project had mapped out around 311.4 sq mi (806.5 km²) of Westeros—including Riverrun (below) and Winterfell (inset)— covering an area of approximately 22,000 x 59,000 blocks. The aim of the project is to use the setting for a role-playing game based on the novels.

LARGEST PLAYABLE GUITAR IN MINECRAFT

On September 27, 2013, *Minecraft* player "disco" used a complex series of redstone circuits to create a mile-long (1.6-km) guitar. Once a user has kickstarted a strum loop of their choice, it's possible to switch chords and perform music by moving between 10 available chord plates.

SUGAR RUSH

ADDICTIVE SWEET TREATS

WOW!

MOST DOWNLOADED MOBILE GAME (CURRENT)

Candy Crush Saga topped the 2014 chart of most downloaded games, according to app experts App Annie. The "match 3" game challenges you to line up three or more identical shapes—in this case, brightly colored candies. King Digital Entertainment, the social games company who created the *Candy Crush* brand, revealed that by January 2014 the addictive game had more than 150 million monthly users.

LARGEST BUBBLEGUM BUBBLE BLOWN

Players of *Candy Crush Saga* will have encountered the fearsome, candy-stealing Bubblegum Troll. Much less terrifying is bubblegum record holder Chad Fell (USA). Chad blew a bubblegum bubble with a diameter of 20 in (50.8 cm)—without using his hands—at Double Springs High School in Winston County, Alabama, on April 24, 2004. The secret of his success, says Chad, is blowing with three pieces of Dubble Bubble gum.

$661 MILLION

Income generated in 2014 by King, the creators of *Candy Crush*. Based in Dublin, Ireland, the company was founded in 2003 and is now one of the biggest developers of Facebook games.

DID YOU KNOW?

On March 26, 2014, the New York Stock Exchange was invaded by giant *Candy Crush* and *Farm Heroes* mascots. The reason? King, the company behind the hit games, had been valued that day at $7.08 billion. Sweet!

MOST POPULAR FACEBOOK APP

Candy Crush Saga continues to sit happily at the top of Facebook's app chart, ahead of *Farm Heroes Saga* and Spotify, according to AppData. The sugary puzzle game is nothing short of a casual-gaming phenomenon, with an estimated 7.7 million daily average users as of August 2014. It brings in $1 million every day in revenues for its creator, King.

LONGEST CHOCOLATE SCULPTURE

This 111-ft 8-in-long (34.05-m) chocolate choo-choo was put on display at Brussels South railroad station in Belgium on November 19, 2012. The tasty train was crafted from Belcolade chocolate by master chocolatier Andrew Farrugia (Malta) as part of Brussels Chocolate Week. A jazz band provided the musical accompaniment on the day, with the keyboard player tinkling away on a grand piano that was also made from chocolate!

FASTEST TIME TO EAT 15 FERRERO ROCHER CHOCOLATES

Crushing candy records is the favorite pastime of Canadian competitive eater "Furious Pete", aka Peter Czerwinski. The champion chomper chowed down 15 Ferrero Rocher chocolates in 2 minutes 22 seconds on October 24, 2014. He also holds one-minute records for eating Creme Eggs (6), Jaffa Cakes (17), and—less sweet— hamburgers (4).

LARGEST PIÑATA

To celebrate the first birthday of M&M's Pretzel Chocolate Candies, a giant piñata was unveiled in New York City on August 4, 2011. The piñata was made in the shape of the Orange M&M "spokescandy" and stuffed with thousands of bags of chocolate pretzels weighing a total of 1,500 lb (680 kg). The finished treat towered 47 ft (14.3 m) high—the equivalent in height to eight fully grown men—and the lucky person chosen to unleash the treats inside was the singer CeeLo Green.

FASTEST TIME TO TYPE A TEXT MESSAGE ON A CELL PHONE USING SWYPE TECHNOLOGY

How things have changed when it comes to keeping in touch … Once upon a time we wrote letters, then came the telegraph, followed by telephones (you know, the kind with wires). Faxes were superseded by e-mails, and then, of course, the **first cell phone** came along in 1973 (see pp. 84–85). Now even the way we text is evolving. Gone are the days of tapping buttons. Thanks to apps such as Swype, you barely have to even lift your finger from the screen. If you've mastered the art of tap-free typing, here's the chance to earn your very own record!

75

Languages supported by the Swype keyboard app, as of September 2015, ranging from Afrikaans to Zulu.

WHAT YOU SWYPING ABOUT?

Did you know the text used in this challenge is a record in its own right? Native to South American rivers, piranhas are deemed the **most ferocious freshwater fish** due to their supersharp, serrated teeth, and the ability for a school of these fish to strip bare an animal as large as a horse within minutes, leaving only its skeleton!

THE RULES

For the full guidelines and to apply, head to **www.guinnessworldrecords.com/blockbusters**.

1. The cell phone used must support touchscreen input and be installed with the Swype app or an equivalent technology.

2. Before the time starts, the contestant can hold the phone in either one or both hands, but their fingers must not be on the keypad.

3. The text to be used for this record is as follows: **The razor-toothed piranhas of the genera Serrasalmus and Pygocentrus are the most ferocious freshwater fish in the world. In reality they seldom attack a human.** The text typed must match exactly the text given above, including spaces, capital letters, and punctuation. During the attempt, text can be corrected and retyped, but the timer will keep running.

4. All typing must be done while holding the device in the hands (e.g. not resting on a table). The challenger may use any combination of fingers to enter the message.

5. The witness in charge of timing should stop their stopwatch when the contestant (believing that the text is completed) holds up the phone at full arm's length.

FASTEST TIME TO TYPE A TEXT MESSAGE...

... on a touchscreen cell phone Marcel Fernandes Filho (Brazil)	17.00 seconds
... on a touchscreen cell phone, blindfolded Mark Encarnación (USA)	25.90 seconds
... on a cell phone Yousef Ahmed Abdul Saboor (Egypt)	29.43 seconds
... on a cell phone, blindfolded Elliot Nicholls (New Zealand)	45.09 seconds

MOST FOLLOWED...

GET TO KNOW THE TWITTERATI

Barack Obama @BarackObama
Four more years. pic.twitter.com/bAJE6Vom   10h
Foto verbergen   ← Antworten   ↻ Retweeten   ★ Favorisieren

PERSON

When it comes to attracting fans on Twitter, Katy Perry (USA) is a bit of a "Dark Horse," with 75,252,403 followers as of September 15, 2015. The US superstar has been the "Queen of Twitter" since 2013, when two weeks after the release of her fourth album *Prism,* her follower count hit 46,555,829—knocking Justin Bieber (below) from the top spot. She has remained the most followed person ever since.

POLITICIAN

Proving that Twitter isn't just about sports icons and pop stars, the third most followed person is US President Barack Obama, with 63,929,740 fans as of September 15, 2015.

It's not the first time that he has shown his commitment to bringing politics into the 21st century. One of his first announcements after taking office was that email would play a much greater part in White House communications, and he became the **first president with regular email access.**

TV PERSONALITY

When not hosting her TV talk show or undertaking movie work (such as voicing amnesiac fish Dory from *Finding Nemo*), Ellen DeGeneres (USA) is keeping online fans entertained. As of September 15, 2015, @TheEllenShow had 47,446,135 followers.

Ellen also set the record for **most retweeted message** when her star-studded selfie from the 2014 Oscars exceeded 1 million retweets in just over an hour.

MALE POP STAR

He might have been overtaken by Katy Perry, but no other male musician has a greater fan base on the social media platform than Justin Bieber (Canada). As of September 15, 2015, his Twitter army of "Beliebers" stood at 67,429,664. That said, in terms of activity, the Canadian far outdoes his American rival, with 29,317 tweets versus Perry's 6,619, as of the same date.

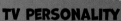

ENTREPRENEUR

With a fortune of $79.2 billion as of March 2015, Microsoft magnate Bill Gates (USA) made enough money from technology and telecommunications to become the world's **richest person**. The entrepreneur has also proved savvy when it comes to social media. With posts focusing on news from the Bill & Melinda Gates Foundation, his Twitter follower count stood at 24,602,423 as of September 15, 2015.

ACTORS

Emma Watson (UK, right) is known for her aptitude at casting spells in *Harry Potter*, but it seems she also knows how to conjure up a huge audience in the Twitterverse. With 19,277,810 followers on her @EmWatson page as of September 15, 2015, she is the **most followed actress**.

Just ahead of her is US film star and comedian Kevin Hart (inset)—best known for movies such as *Get Hard* (2015). With 21,518,475 followers as of the same date, he is the **most followed actor** overall.

500 MILLION

Estimated number of tweets sent every day among the site's 316 million monthly active users, according to Twitter data from June 30, 2015.

WOW!

ATHLETES

As well as being the **most "liked" person on Facebook**, Portuguese soccer star Cristiano Ronaldo also reigns supreme over all other athletes on Twitter, with 37,831,159 followers as of September 15, 2015. As you'd expect, the majority of his tweets focus on soccer, but he also offers endorsements and glimpses into his home life.

As well as boasting the **highest earnings in a tennis career (female)**—$66,211,528, as of March 9, 2015—US tennis ace Serena Williams is also the **most followed female athlete**, with 5,379,139 followers.

MOST LIKED...

GIVING YOUR FAVORITES A THUMBS-UP

DECEASED CELEBRITY ON FACEBOOK

Music legend Michael Jackson (USA) may have passed away in 2009, but that hasn't stopped fans flocking to his Facebook page. As of September 16, 2015, he had received 75,926,444 "likes"—more than any other deceased celebrity, and, in fact, the seventh most liked overall.

MALE MUSICIAN ON FACEBOOK

With 92,411,319 "likes" as of September 16, 2015, Eminem (USA) is the most popular male musician on the world's **largest social media site**. Born Marshall Bruce Mathers III, Eminem is not just the **fastest-selling rapper**—*The Marshall Mathers LP* sold 1.76 million copies in its first week in the USA in May 2000—he's also one of the fastest rappers: his single "Rap God" packed in 1,560 lyrics, the **most words in a hit single**.

SPORTS TEAM ON FACEBOOK

No other sports team has amassed more "likes" than FC Barcelona of Spain. As of September 16, 2015, the squad had received the thumbs-up from 86,831,164 supporters, putting them just ahead of their main rivals, Real Madrid CF, on 84,349,996. Pictured are some of the Barcelona team celebrating a goal against Juventus in the 2015 UEFA Champions League Final in Berlin, Germany.

FACEBOOK POST

As of September 16, 2015, the most "likes" received for a single Facebook post is 7,801,879, for an update by the movie actor Vin Diesel (USA) on December 6, 2013. In the emotional post, Diesel remembers his *Furious 7* costar Paul Walker, who had died the week before in a car crash. For more on this blockbusting movie, see p. 47.

IMAGE ON INSTAGRAM

A photograph of fashion model and TV personality Kendall Jenner (USA)—posted in May 2015—had been "liked" more than 3.1 million times as of September 2015. Jenner, who shot to fame following her appearance on *Keeping Up with the Kardashians*, is the daughter of TV star Kris Jenner and record-breaking Olympic athlete Bruce (now Caitlyn) Jenner—who broke records for **most points in a decathlon** in 1975–76.

MOST "LIKES" FOR A FOOD/BEVERAGE BRAND ON FACEBOOK

Coca-Cola had a staggering 92,953,854 "likes" on its Facebook page as of September 16, 2015, more than any other food or drinks brand. The next highest contender in this category is McDonald's, with 58,878,991 "likes."

81,604,986 "LIKES"
for Shakira's nearest rival on Facebook, Rihanna—the second most "liked" female on the social media site.

WOW!

FEMALE ON FACEBOOK

The first celebrity to attract 100 million "likes" on an official Facebook fan page was Colombian vocalist Shakira (b. Shakira Mebarak Ripoll), who reached the landmark in July 2014. As of September 16, 2015, the "Hips Don't Lie" star—whose page is regularly updated with videos, news, and photos—had 102,721,139 "likes."

The only other human being with more "likes" than Shakira is footballer Cristiano Ronaldo (Portugal), with 106,464,840 as of the same date.

MOST WATCHED

ONLINE VIDEOS THAT WENT VIRAL

WOW!

LARGEST VIDEO-SHARING SITE

The **first YouTube video** was posted to the site in 2005 by one of the company's cofounders, Jawed Karim (Germany/USA). When Karim uploaded his "Me at the Zoo" clip, it's unlikely anyone could have foreseen the platform's runaway success. Bought out by Google for $1.65 billion in 2006, it has since been riding high as the undisputed king of online video.

In 2015, the web giant boasted more than 1 billion unique users each month, with in excess of 6 billion hours of video watched. YouTube estimates that more than 100 hours of video are added every single minute!

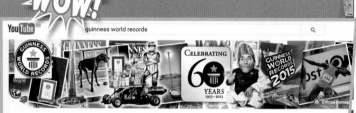

guinness world records

Guinness World Records

Home   Videos   Playlists   Channels   Discussion   About

Guinness World Records YouTube Channel
95,589 views 3 months ago

Welcome to the official Guinness World Records YouTube channel! If you're looking for videos featuring the world's tallest, shortest, fastest, longest, oldest and most incredible things on the planet, you're in the right place.

Subscribe for more: http://bit.ly/subscribetoGWR

Each Monday, we bring you jaw dropping records both old and new from our Guinness World Records video ...
Read more

0:57 / 1:05

MOST VIEWED ONLINE VIDEO

Talking of unforeseen successes, who could ever have predicted that Korean pop star PSY, with his "Gangnam Style" music video, would smash all-time view counts?

Having claimed the record for **first video to receive 1 billion views** in 2012, the most watched video continues to storm ahead of all its rivals, with 2,395,264,885 views as of August 19, 2015.

As if that wasn't enough success, PSY's 2013 single "Gentleman" achieved the **most viewed video in 24 hours**, watched 38,409,306 times.

MOST CONCURRENT VIEWS FOR A LIVE EVENT ON YOUTUBE

Teetering 127,852 ft (38,969.4 m) above Earth, preparing to jump, must have been a pretty epic experience for Austrian skydiver Felix Baumgartner—and as it turns out, it made for pretty epic viewing, too.

On October 14, 2012, Baumgartner not only set several high-altitude records, including **highest manned balloon flight** and **first person to break the sound barrier in freefall**, but also pushed the envelope for online video. According to Google, an audience of 8 million almost crashed YouTube's servers to glimpse his historic leap.

MOST VIEWED SCI-FI MOVIE TRAILER

More than a year ahead of the much-anticipated release of *Star Wars: The Force Awakens* in movie theaters, a trailer was posted to YouTube that got sci-fi fans in a frenzy. As of August 19, 2015, it had been seen a staggering 70,782,332 times.

Although lasting only 1 minute 30 seconds, the teaser packs in plenty of classic *Star Wars* action, with stormtroopers, X-wings, and TIE fighters, plus the iconic *Millennium Falcon* (left). A second snippet became the **most viewed movie trailer in 24 hours** (see p. 16).

(see p. 16)

15,484,762

Views for an official *Star Wars Battlefront* trailer, as of September 10, 2015. Premiered at the E3 gaming conference in June 2015, the teaser shows an epic multiplayer battle against AT-ATs on the icy planet of Hoth.

MOST LIVE STREAMS FOR A SINGLE EVENT

Felix Baumgartner may hold the record for most YouTube viewers at a given moment (see left), but over the course of a streamed live event, British royals Prince William and Catherine Middleton accumulated 72 million views during their wedding on April 29, 2011. Of the 188 countries who tuned in as "virtual guests," the top five were the UK, the USA, Italy, Germany, and France, according to YouTube.

FIRST PERSON WITH A MILLION FOLLOWERS ON TWITCH

YouTube is far from the only online video hub. The **largest video site dedicated to gaming** is Twitch, which focuses on entertaining commentaries, walk-through guides, and live gaming events. YouTube has "PewDiePie" (see p. 173), but the **most popular Twitch broadcaster** is Tom Cassell (UK), aka "Syndicate." He surpassed the million-follower milestone in August 2014, and as of August 19, 2015, his count stood at 2,016,331.

(see p. 173)

APPS & ONLINE

RICHE$T YOUTUBER$

YOUTUBE'S HIGHEST-EARNING ...

Whatever its focus, from gaming to music, or unboxing (such as Blucollection, pictured below), Social Blade estimates YouTube channel earnings based on the money generated for every thousand ad views. The reason the range is so big is because costs per view vary drastically across platforms and countries. It's also worth noting that these figures don't take into account the hefty 45 percent or so cut taken by Google and nonmonetized views.

OVERALL CONTRIBUTOR

According to Social Blade's calculations, nobody on YouTube is earning more than "DisneyCollectorBR," aka "FunToyzCollector"— an anonymous female contributor from Brazil earning an estimated $12.45 million per year. The channel is at the forefront of the "unboxing" trend, where toys and other products are unpackaged and discussed. To the left is a table of the leading unboxing YouTubers, with "DisneyCollectorBR" reigning supreme at No. 1.

TOP 5 YOUTUBE UNBOXERS

1. DisneyCollectorBR
$12.45 million

2. Blucollection
$6.11 million

3. DisneyCarToys
$5.47 million

4. ItsBabyBigMouth
$4.83 million

5. TheEducVideos
$4.78 million

Source: Social Blade (mean average); February 2015

5,099,189
Subscribers to the "DisneyCollectorBR" channel (below), as of August 2015. The unboxer also boasts more than 7.6 billion views across all of her videos since joining YouTube in April 2011.

EDUCATIONAL CONTRIBUTOR

As of February 2015, YouTube stats expert Social Blade estimated that the "LittleBabyBum" channel—best known for its animated nursery rhymes, such as "Wheels on the Bus"—was earning in the region of $845,500 to $13.5 million annually. This represents a mean average of $7.17 million. Founded in 2011, the channel is managed by British animation and app-making team Derek Holder and his wife. As of August 2015, it had attracted 3,396,263 subscribers.

WOW!

GAMING CONTRIBUTOR

It's no surprise that "PewDiePie," the **most subscribed-to YouTube channel**—38,746,465, as of August 19, 2015—is a top earner. According to Social Blade, "PewDiePie," aka Felix Arvid Ulf Kjellberg of Sweden, had annual earnings of $1.2 million to $18.9 million, which is a mean average of $10.05 million. His smash-hit channel mainly posts playthroughs of games with humorous commentary, focusing on indie titles including *McPixel* (2012) and *Goat Simulator* (2014). Below, he receives his GWR certificate, which he attributes to his "Bro Army."

MINECRAFT CONTRIBUTOR

While YouTube's **highest-earning gaming contributor** (left) touches on *Minecraft* now and then, there are many channels completely dedicated to the blockbusting phenomenon (see pp. 158–61). King of these in terms of income, according to Social Blade, is "PopularMMOs," with estimated earnings of $6.37 million per year. This puts it ahead of other *Minecraft*-mad channels, such as "stampylonghead" and "TheDiamondMinecart."

GOOGLE

THE SEARCH IS OVER ...

Google

LARGEST SEARCH ENGINE

Google no longer publishes its index size, but in terms of the number of searches, it is certainly the most popular online search tool. According to Internet Live Stats, the Google search engine now processes an average of at least 40,000 queries every second—that's more than 3.5 billion searches per day and 1.2 trillion per year.

HIGHEST FREEFALL PARACHUTE JUMP

While YouTube's live stream of Felix Baumgartner received record audiences (see p. 170), Google's senior vice president Alan Eustace (USA) claimed the title on October 24, 2014, out of the media spotlight. Carried to an altitude of 135,898 ft (41,422 m) above New Mexico by a helium balloon, his descent back to Earth lasted just over 15 minutes.

GREATEST AGGREGATE DISTANCE BY A DRIVERLESS CAR FLEET

In 2012, Nevada issued the world's first autonomous vehicle license to a Toyota Prius fitted with "Google Chauffeur" software. The self-driving car gathers data from GPS positioning, detailed maps of the local area, LIDAR (laser radar scanner) technology that visualizes the surroundings in 3D (inset), and a number of other sensors. The software is capable of driving fully autonomously, but Google mandates that a human takes control through urban roads, as well as at the start and end of a journey. On June 3, 2015, Google announced the car had passed the landmark figure of 1 million miles (1.6 million km) of automated driving.

FIRST SMART CONTACT LENS

In 2014, Google X—the company's technology research and development arm—unveiled a prototype contact lens that has the potential to save lives. Thanks to a built-in tiny microchip, hair-thin sensor, and an antenna, it can monitor the blood-sugar levels of diabetics via tear fluid on the surface of the eyes. If glucose ever dips too low or rises too high, the lens can send instant alerts to a cell phone.

LARGEST ONLINE INTERACTIVE MAP

Earth Viewer was acquired by Google in 2004 and relaunched as Google Earth a year later. The virtual 3D replica of our planet, created from satellite data, represents the majority of land at 49-ft (15-m) resolution, though points of interest are as high as 6-in (15-cm) resolution. Special features have since mapped out areas beyond *terra firma*, including Google Ocean, Google Sky, and even Google Mars.

FIRST GOOGLE+ HANGOUT IN SPACE

Google.com is even the go-to website *off* our planet. On October 18, 2012, the search engine teamed up with the Japanese space agency to set up a 20-minute chat between astronaut Akihiko Hoshide on board the *International Space Station* and a group of students on Earth. The technology had previously been used by astronauts privately, but this was the first public Hangout.

FIRST "SMART GLASSES"

The prototype Google Glass entered stores from May 2014 to January 2015, offering a new take on augmented reality. Running on Google's own Android 4.4, a 640-x-480-pixel display beamed images—from cooking videos to cycling routes—directly into the wearer's right eye, controlled by speech and touch commands.

Google is currently working on the second-generation Google Glass, having stated that it will only be released when "perfect."

WOW!

1 KIM KARDASHIAN
44,195,314

In August 2015, Kim Kardashian (USA) took the **most followed Instagrammer** crown from singer Beyoncé (see No. 2), proving that more and more people find the photo site the perfect way of "keeping up with" their favorite reality TV star. Kim's springboard to fame, the fly-on-the-wall series *Keeping Up with the Kardashians* (*KUwtK*), follows the everyday life of the Kardashian-Jenner family and has proven a smash hit since 2007. Her page is largely given to "selfies," red-carpet events, and family shots with rapper husband Kanye West and daughter North West.

2 BEYONCÉ
44,048,413

Former Destiny's Child member Beyoncé Knowles (USA) was "Queen of Instagram" until Kim Kardashian's fans ousted her, but she can still take consolation in having the **most followers for a musician**. Her snaps and videos feature everything from fashion shoots and family vacations to flowers and even one with the *Mona Lisa* in Paris. Ooh la la!

3 TAYLOR SWIFT
43,769,600

The next most popular musician is "Shake It Off" star Taylor Swift (USA). In 2015, she complained to Apple about its plan to offer a free trial to its new streaming service, Apple Music, during which no royalties would be paid to artists. After widespread criticism, the tech giant backed down a week later. An online army of supporters sure can come in handy!

4 SELENA GOMEZ
41,997,154

Making her breakthrough in Disney sitcom *Wizards of Waverly Place* in 2007, actor-turned-pop star Selena Gomez (USA) has clearly worked her magic in the realm of social media, too. Her Instagram portfolio is largely made up of various selfies—often taken with friends and other Hollywood celebs.

5 ARIANA GRANDE
41,841,247

Pictured above with her beagle-Chihuahua, Toulouse—a regular guest star on her Instagram page—Ariana Grande (USA) is another vocalist who likes to shoot and share with the world. Grande spent most of 2015 on her Honeymoon Tour, so many of her posts were taken on the road or at her sell-out concerts.

6 JUSTIN BIEBER
37,149,373

In a female-dominated Top 10, Canadian singer Justin Bieber is by far the **most followed male on Instagram**. As well as posting about tattoos, skateboarding, and sneakers, in 2015 he also ran a campaign in which famous faces held signs promoting his new single "What Do You Mean?", which would go on to become his first Billboard Hot 100 No. 1.

7 KENDALL JENNER
35,536,402

The second *Kardashians* star in our lineup, fashion model Kendall Jenner (USA) is some way behind her half-sister (No. 1). But she can take some solace in the fact that one of her selfies claimed the record for **most liked image on Instagram** from Kim in May 2015 (see p. 169).

8 KYLIE JENNER
33,881,537

Hot on the heels of her elder sister Kendall is fellow reality TV celebrity and socialite Kylie Jenner (USA). It's fitting that their Instagram follower counts should be so close considering how much the siblings have done together in recent years. They have launched their own clothing line—Kendall & Kylie—and even cowrote a sci-fi novel, *Rebels: City of Indra*, which hit stores in 2014.

9 NICKI MINAJ
32,392,246

Trinidad-born singer-songwriter Nicki Minaj might be the sixth highest-ranked musician in terms of followers, but she is by far the most active Instagrammer in this roundup. Compared with her fellow singers, her account had 3,241 posts as of August 26, 2015; Beyoncé had 1,084, Swift had 666, Gomez had 984, Grande had 1,789, and Bieber had 2,336.

10 KHLOÉ KARDASHIAN
30,645,097

Rounding up Instagram's elite, TV personality Khloé Kardashian (USA, left) takes the power family's domination to 40% of the Top 10! In 2014–15, she starred with her sister in *KUwtK* spin-off *Kourtney & Khloé Take the Hamptons*. In the above snap, the siblings get beaten in a tongue-sticking-out contest at the zoo!

Data taken from socialblade.com and correct as of August 26, 2015

TOYS

CHALLENGE

A RECORD TO SET YOUR SIGHTS ON!

MOST TIMES TO HIT A TARGET WITH A FOAM-BULLET GUN IN ONE MINUTE

Fancy yourself as something of a sharp-shooting secret agent with a foam-bullet gun? Well, if you think you've got speed, accuracy, and plenty of patience, this is the challenge for you. Your mission, if you choose to accept it, is to fire as many darts at a target in 60 seconds—but be warned, only the bullets that stay stuck will count toward your total. There's no requirement to hit the bull's-eye for this record, but it goes without saying that this will earn you extra kudos!

MOST TARGETS HIT ...

... in one minute with plungers (human targets)	
Gerhard Donie (Germany)	15
... in one minute with basketballs	
Luis Scola (Argentina) & Liu Xiaoyu (China)	16
... in two minutes with tennis serves (blindfolded)	
Ashrita Furman (USA)	20
... in three minutes with golf shots	
Federico Ranelletti (Italy)	20

THE RULES

For the full guidelines and to apply, head to **www.guinnessworldrecords.com/blockbusters**.

1. Any external single-fire foam-bullet gun that fires Velcro- or suction-tip projectiles may be used.

2. "External single-fire" means that the gun must be reloaded manually after each shot. The first bullet can be preloaded; the others can be lined up next to the participant.

3. The target must be circular and no larger than 9.8 in (25 cm) in diameter. It must also be able to retain the projectiles (i.e., so that they stick).

4. The target must be placed a minimum of 16 ft 5 in (5 m) away from the participant at any height. This distance must be clearly marked on the ground where the attempt takes place. The participant must remain behind the line at all times. Any bullets fired while the claimant stepped over the line will be deducted.

5. Bullets must remain stuck to the target for at least 5 seconds after the initial minute is up.

6. The full attempt must be recorded and submitted as evidence.

LARGEST OUTDOOR AND SPORTS TOY BRAND (CURRENT)

One of the biggest names in the world of foam-dart blasters is NERF, so it's little wonder that the US company—owned by Hasbro—is currently on top. According to market research by Euromonitor International, the range, which also includes water pistols, flying disks, balls, and other outdoor toys, brought in around $620,700,000 in 2014.

K'NEX

FAST AND FURIOUS CONSTRUCTION

55 SECONDS
Estimated time that the *Bloodhound SSC* will need to go from 0 to 1,000 mph, with the 500–1,000-mph stretch taking just 17 seconds!

LARGEST K'NEX SCULPTURE

With construction toys such as K'NEX, the only limit on what we can build is our own imagination. Many of us will have tinkered with K'NEX at some point, recreating everything from theme park rides to robots, but it's unlikely you've ever created anything on this scale … an actual-size replica of the *Bloodhound Supersonic Car*. The dimensions of this amazing sculpture, constructed by the BLOODHOUND SSC RBLI K'NEX Build Team (UK), are 43 ft 10.7 in long, 8 ft wide, and 12 ft 8.3 in high (13.38 x 2.44 m x 3.87 m), as confirmed on August 26, 2014.

THE REAL *BLOODHOUND*

This mega model of a jet-powered supercar is pretty cool ... but what its inspiration is aiming to achieve in 2016 is cooler still!

Can you imagine hurtling the length of four-and-a-half football fields in just one second? That's exactly what it's hoped the *Bloodhound SSC* can achieve in its quest to smash the current **land-speed record**.

Set in 1997 by Andy Green (UK), driving the *Thrust SSC*, the top speed stands at 763.035 mph. But, far from resting on his laurels, Green is once again taking to the wheel to try to break the 1,000-mph barrier.

Work began back in 2008, and *Bloodhound* is due to make its debut during runway tests in late 2015. The record attempt is set to take place in South Africa in summer 2016.

350,000 K'NEX PIECES went into the construction of this record-breaking sculpture, along with 1,280 hours of assembly time.

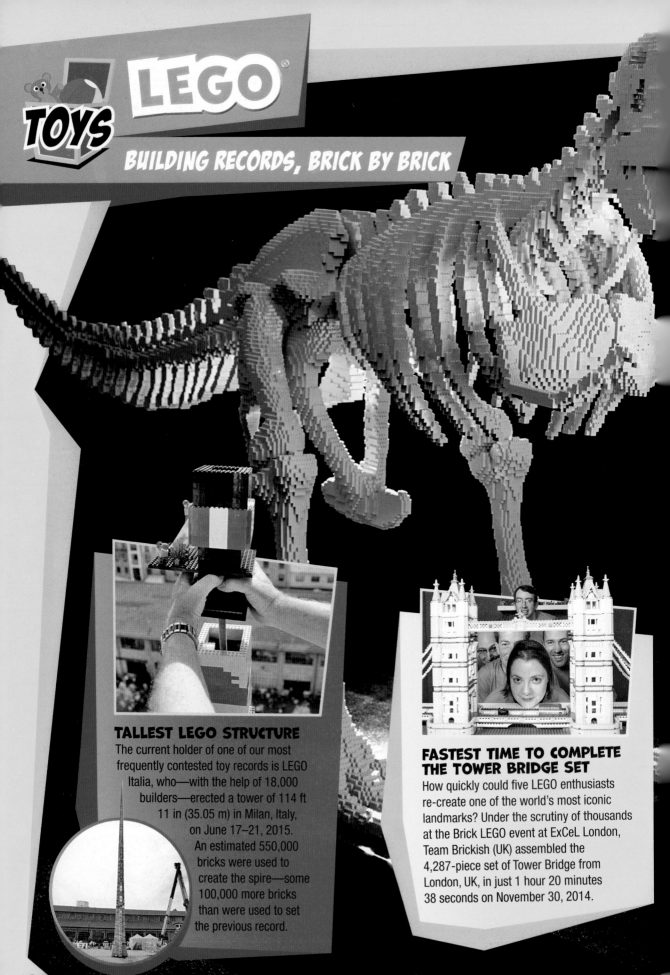

LEGO®

BUILDING RECORDS, BRICK BY BRICK

TALLEST LEGO STRUCTURE

The current holder of one of our most frequently contested toy records is LEGO Italia, who—with the help of 18,000 builders—erected a tower of 114 ft 11 in (35.05 m) in Milan, Italy, on June 17–21, 2015. An estimated 550,000 bricks were used to create the spire—some 100,000 more bricks than were used to set the previous record.

FASTEST TIME TO COMPLETE THE TOWER BRIDGE SET

How quickly could five LEGO enthusiasts re-create one of the world's most iconic landmarks? Under the scrutiny of thousands at the Brick LEGO event at ExCeL London, Team Brickish (UK) assembled the 4,287-piece set of Tower Bridge from London, UK, in just 1 hour 20 minutes 38 seconds on November 30, 2014.

LARGEST COLLECTION OF *STAR WARS* LEGO SETS

Jon Jessesen (Norway), a mega-fan of both LEGO and *Star Wars*, had to call on both his passions to achieve this feat. As of January 1, 2015, he was the proud owner of no fewer than 378 unopened *Star Wars* LEGO sets, as well as the complete 646-strong army of LEGO *Star Wars* Minifigures (pictured above right).

80,020 BRICKS

Number of LEGO pieces used by Sawaya to construct his *Tyrannosaurus rex*. By comparison, he estimates a life-size human model uses around 20,000 bricks.

MOST EXPENSIVE LEGO BRICK

A super-rare 2 x 4 LEGO piece made of 14-carat gold sold for $12,500 to an anonymous buyer in 2012. Designed as gifts for long-term LEGO employees, very few of the blingy bricks were ever manufactured—making them even more desirable.

GUINNESS WORLD RECORDS

CERTIFICATE

The largest skeleton made from interlocking plastic bricks consists of 80,020 pieces of LEGO, the *Dinosaur Skeleton* was created by Nathan Sawaya (USA) and forms part of "The Art of the Brick" touring exhibition

OFFICIALLY AMAZING

RECORD HOLDER

WOW!

LARGEST LEGO SKELETON

Former lawyer Nathan Sawaya (USA) has taken the humble LEGO brick to the world of fine art with phenomenal success. By far the largest sculpture on show in his exhibition *The Art of the Brick* is this life-size reproduction of a *T. rex* skeleton, which stretches 20 ft (6.1 m) from snout to tail! Nathan says that it took him a whole summer to build it.

LARGEST MINIFIGURE MADE WITH BALLOONS

LEGO Minifigures, as their name suggests, are fairly small—typically around 1.7 in (4.5 cm) in height. But this monster, built using 1,985 modeling balloons by Larry Moss (USA) and his team, stood a mighty 19 ft 8 in (6 m)! The not-so-mini figure—150 times larger than the standard size—made a big impression at 2014's Brick LEGO event in London, UK.

FOR MORE LEGO, KEEP READING ...

TOYS

LEGO®

THE TOY BRICK GOES DIGITAL

WOW!

MOST PROLIFIC VIDEO GAME SERIES BASED ON A TOY

No other toy has inspired more video games than the humble plastic building brick, with 65 LEGO titles released as of July 21, 2015. The very first in 1997 was Mindscape's *LEGO Island* and the most recent is the Warner Bros. game *LEGO Jurassic World* (2015, below), launched with the movie. *Jurassic World* is the 27th LEGO-themed game created by TT Games, which— combined with a *Transformers* video game they released in 2007—makes TT the **most prolific developer of toy video games** overall.

20 DINOSAURS

As well as human characters, you are also able to play as the real stars of *Jurassic World*: the dinosaurs! Unlockable species include Triceratops, Velociraptor, and everyone's favorite, the *T. rex* (below).

MOST CRITICALLY ACCLAIMED TOY-BASED VIDEO GAME

Audience satisfaction doesn't necessarily always align with sales figures … LucasArts' *LEGO Star Wars: The Complete Saga* (2007) is the **best-selling LEGO video game**, but it isn't the most admired. That plaudit goes to its 2006 predecessor, *LEGO Star Wars II: The Original Trilogy*, which had a GameRankings rating of 86.83%, as of July 21, 2015.

FIRST LEGO GAME MADE ENTIRELY OUT OF BRICKS

The LEGO Movie Videogame, released by Warner Bros. alongside the eponymous film in February 2014, was the first LEGO game in which everything was constructed out of bricks, from buildings and furniture to vehicles. "We challenged ourselves to introduce a new element never-before-seen," explained Tom Stone from developer TT Games.

MOST PLAYABLE CHARACTERS IN AN ACTION-ADVENTURE GAME

If you're the kind of gamer who quickly gets bored of always playing as the same character, then *LEGO Marvel Super Heroes* (2013) is one for you. As well as 180 iconic heroes, villains, and sidekicks, from Ant-Man to Yellowjacket, an in-game customization system allows for more than a billion different configurations of the characters, so you can create your own unique figures, too.

FASTEST COMPLETION OF *LEGO HARRY POTTER: YEAR 1*

For many people, time at school seems to pass slowly … But Norwegian speed-runner Marius Losvik virtually "apparated" through Year 1 at Hogwarts in *LEGO Harry Potter: Years 1–4* (2010), finishing the section in just 50 minutes 6 seconds. The full game covers the events of the first four movies in the wizarding odyssey.

CHALLENGE

LEGO® IN A GALAXY FAR, FAR AWAY ...

FASTEST TIME TO BUILD THE LEGO *STAR WARS MILLENNIUM FALCON* MICROFIGHTER

Do you consider yourself a Master Builder like Emmet from *The LEGO Movie*? Think you can put together LEGO bricks quicker than Anakin Skywalker can draw his lightsaber? Now's your chance to prove it. You're welcome to practice building your mini *Millennium Falcon* as many times as you want before going for the record, but note that when it comes to the attempt all the pieces must be separated and clearly shown at the start of your recorded video (like the top image opposite).

THE RULES

For the full guidelines and to apply, head to **www.guinnessworldrecords.com/blockbusters**.

1. This record uses the LEGO *Star Wars* 75030: *Millennium Falcon* microfighter kit exclusively and should be attempted only by an individual.

2. All pieces must be securely and correctly fitted, as per the instruction manual. No form of adhesive may be used.

3. Although the order in which the kit is completed is up to you, we recommend that the sequence provided by LEGO in the box (or on the website) is followed to be sure that no pieces are skipped. It is acceptable to rebuild during the attempt, but the clock will continue running.

4. When the challenger believes they are finished, they must put down the model and raise their hand to signal that the timer should be stopped.

5. The entire attempt must be filmed and be clearly visible for GWR to assess. An experienced timekeeper (e.g. an official from a local sports club) should time the event and corroborate the evidence, along with one other impartial witness.

TOP TRIVIA

 The *Millennium Falcon* has gone by many names, including *Stellar Envoy*, *Fickle Flyer*, and *Gone to Pieces*.

 The *Falcon*'s owner, Han Solo, won the spacecraft after a lucky hand in a card game called "sabacc."

 In the real world, the Full Scale *Millennium Falcon* Project, conceived in 2005 and led by Chris Lee (USA), is in the process of building a 1:1-scale replica of the spaceship.

POKÉMON

MONSTERS IN YOUR POCKET

21.5 BILLION
Pokémon trading cards sold in 74 countries; in 2002, the Pokémon franchise was valued at more than $26 billion!

MOST WINS OF THE POKÉMON VIDEO GAME WORLD CHAMPIONSHIP

On August 11, 2012, 19-year-old Ray Rizzo (USA) defeated rival Wolfe Glick in the Pokémon Video Game World Championship final. This was the third year in a row that he had taken the title. "Hydreigon is my favorite and, in my opinion, the best Dragon," revealed Ray. "Rotom-W was the Pokémon I used the least."

TOP 5
POKÉMON VIDEO GAMES

1. *Red / Green / Blue*
31.37 million sold

2. *Gold / Silver*
23.10 million sold

3. *Diamond / Pearl*
18.23 million sold

4. *Ruby / Sapphire*
15.85 million sold

5. *Black / White*
15.12 million sold

Source: VGChartz (August 2015)

GUINNESS WORLD RECORDS CERTIFICATE

The most successful family of videogame Pokémon players is the Arnolds of Frankfort, Illinois, USA. Five members of whom have taken part in officially-sanctioned world championships as of July 2011.

LARGEST COLLECTION OF POKÉMON MEMORABILIA

Lisa Courtney (UK) truly lives up to the tag line "Gotta catch 'em all!" having amassed 14,410 items of Pokémon memorabilia—mostly plush toys. She started collecting after being bullied at school—"Pokémon was the only thing that made me feel happy," Lisa says—and has now been collecting for nearly 20 years, with no plans to stop. "There's always something new to collect!"

WOW!

MOST SUCCESSFUL POKÉMON-PLAYING FAMILY

Pokémon's family-friendly charm is confirmed by the record-breaking Arnold family from Frankfort, Illinois. Five of the family—Ryan, mom Linda, Ryan's twin David, dad Glenn, and youngest child Grace (pictured left to right)—have all taken part in official *Pokémon* video-game world championships. "Families that play together, stay together," as the saying goes, and when they're not competing at *Pokémon*, the Arnolds play together in a marching band!

CATCH MORE POKÉMON OVER THE PAGE!

MOST MOVIE SPIN-OFFS FROM A VIDEO GAME

It isn't just a smash hit on TV—as of July 2015, *Pokémon* can also boast 19 feature-length animated films. The series' debut, *Pokémon: The First Movie: Mewtwo Strikes Back* (1998, right), is also the **highest-grossing animated movie based on a video game**, pulling in $163,644,662 globally. Its success was helped by movie theaters handing out rare Pokémon trading cards at the screenings.

82 EPISODES

in the Indigo League (1997–99), the first ever Pokémon TV series, making it the longest season. The shortest series is Black & White: Adventures in Unova and Beyond (2013–14), with just 22 episodes.

SUPERLATIVE POKÉMON

Although the original Pokédex was limited to 151 Pokémon, across subsequent generations the family had multiplied to 720 species—and counting—as of July 2015. From Water and Fire to Ghost and Psychic, the strengths and weaknesses of the 18 different "types" vary widely, but here are a handful of record-breaking Pokémon that stand out from the crowd.

FIRST POKÉMON

Despite being #112 in the original Pokédex, Rhydon was the first character created by Poké-artist Ken Sugimori.

HEAVIEST POKÉMON

The mascot for *Pokémon Ruby* (2002), Groudon weighs in at a whopping 2,094 lb (950 kg).

SMALLEST POKÉMON

You have to look extra hard to spot electric-bug Joltik, who stands just 4 in (10 cm) tall.

FASTEST POKÉMON

The Usain Bolt of the Pokémon world is Psychic-type Deoxys, with an unrivaled speed rating of 180.

WOW!

LONGEST-RUNNING TV SERIES INSPIRED BY A VIDEO GAME

The hugely popular *Pokémon* anime series was first screened on Japanese television on April 1, 1997, with the pilot episode "Pokémon, I Choose You!" Since then, the show has been in constant production, clocking up a monster 884 episodes across 18 seasons, as of July 30, 2015.

DID YOU KNOW?

Pokémon aren't the only Japanese monsters battling it out for kids' affection. Released just after Pokémon, Digimon—aka "Digital Monsters"—have also shot to fame in movies, TV series, and games, though their origins lie in Tamagotchi-style toys. Above is Hououmon from 2014 fighting game *Digimon All-Star Rumble*.

$70

The most money that Susan has ever paid for one of her collectables—for a vintage caterpillar Slinky pull-toy. She suspects that its actual value is considerably higher.

LARGEST COLLECTION OF SLINKYS

If you thought that Slinky toys only came in one style, you'd better think again. Susan Suazo from New Mexico owns 1,054 different Slinkys, as verified on October 25, 2014—and not one of them is a duplicate!

Susan's passion began when she was 14 years old and working at her uncle's restaurant, where there was a vending machine selling the toys: "By the time that summer was over, I had emptied the machine twice and made friends with the vendor who filled it up!" Susan displays the majority of her collection in a dedicated "Slinky Room" at home, although she also keeps two on her desk at work as "stress relievers."

AN INTERVIEW WITH:
SUSAN SUAZO

Shown here in her Slinky Room, Susan sprung into action to tell us a little more about her unusual collection.

How often do you play with your Slinkys?
I'd say I play with some Slinky or another daily. Most times, I begin [picking up] a Slinky for display manipulation, but it always turns into playing. I even have Slinkys that talk, so I occasionally turn one of those on to see if it has something new to say!

Do you have a sure-fire technique for making sure a Slinky makes it to the bottom of the stairs?
You have to match the diameter of the Slinky to the width of the stairs.
From a physics standpoint, you can't push a 3-in [7.6-cm] Slinky down an 8-in-tread [20.3-cm] staircase, since after one flip, it remains on the same step. As long as the "run" of the stair is only about an inch bigger than the diameter of the toy, the Slinky performs famously all the way to the bottom.

Is there a "Holy Grail" of Slinkys you would love to get hold of?
I was told of a unit in the shape of a small wooden barrel—big enough to fit a small child—similar to those used to store wine or liquor. The one I was told of was donated to a day care center when its owner moved. It would be a dream to have something very large like that in my collection.

RETRO PLAYTIME

TOYS

WHO SAYS THE CLASSICS CAN'T STILL BE FUN?

LARGEST CHESS PIECE

Potter fans will recall that life-or-death game of giant chess the characters play in *Harry Potter and the Sorcerer's Stone*. Well, this king chess piece isn't out to kill, but it certainly is big. Standing 16 ft 7 in (5.07 m) tall and with a base of 6 ft 8 in (2.04 m), the colossal sculpture was created by the Gitok school in Belgium in aid of charity. Its status as "kingpin" was verified on April 4, 2014.

SMALLEST RUBIK'S CUBE

Anyone who's ever tried to solve a Rubik's Cube will know it's no mean feat, but imagine trying to complete one smaller than a sugar cube! This tiny puzzle, which is fully functional, was created by Evgeniy Grigoriev (Russia) and its sides measure just 0.39 in (10 mm). This bettered his previous record-breaking Rubik's Cube by 0.08 in (2 mm).

ACTUAL SIZE

LARGEST TWISTER MAT

Students at the University of Twente in the Netherlands played this scaled-up party game for about an hour on September 1, 2011. Measuring 171 ft 1 in x 140 ft 1 in (52.15 m x 42.70 m), it could have accommodated 900 standard Twister mats. It came with a suitably huge spinner (left).

WOW!

4,160 PLAYERS took part in the **largest game of Twister**. The game took place at the University of Massachusetts at Amherst on May 2, 1987, and was won by Allison Culler.

LARGEST MONOPOLY BOARD

In 2012, De Eindhovense School in the Netherlands took on the challenge of creating a supersize version of the iconic property-buying game Monopoly. Covering 2,421 sq ft (225 m²), the enormous board also set the overall record for **largest board game**. It even featured its own set of scaled-up houses and hotels (a few of which are shown above).

FASTEST TIME TO BUILD A 30-LEVEL JENGA TOWER

Steady hands and steely nerves were needed when Jenga-loving brothers Tyler and Ryan Measel (both USA) took on this record on June 7, 2014. Keeping to official rules, the siblings moved the 36 required blocks to complete the 30th story of their tower in 2 minutes 51.04 seconds, smashing the sub-three-minute target they had set themselves.

TOYS POGO!

PUTTING A SPRING IN YOUR STEP

TALLEST POGO STICK

When it comes to pogo sticks, one name leaps to mind. Prodigious pogo performer Fred Grzybowski (USA) unveiled a 9-ft 6.5-in-tall (2.91-m) pogo stick at the Toronto International BuskerFest in Canada on August 7, 2011. And as per the Guinness World Records guidelines, the supersize stick was usable, as demonstrated by Fred in this photo.

MOST PEOPLE PERFORMING SYNCHRONIZED BACKFLIPS ON POGO STICKS

On July 2, 2014, at the Pogopalooza Pittsburgh event at Point State Park in Pennsylvania, 15 pogo athletes performed a simultaneous backflip. Flippin' impressive!

MOST BOUNCES IN A POGO-STICK MARATHON

James Roumeliotis (USA) bounced a spine-crunching 206,864 times in a pogo-sticking endurance marathon on July 29, 2011. The superlative springer bounced for 20 hours 13 minutes at Pogopalooza 8 in Costa Mesa, California, and smashed his own record of 186,152, set back in 2007.

WOW!

POGOPALOOZA

The sport of extreme pogo-sticking is governed by XPogo, who stage a touring Pogo World Championships known as Pogopalooza. These family-friendly events are a celebration of all things pogo. They attract the world's best pogo-stickers, who compete in freestyle events and show off their skills in exhibitions. They can also take a crack at the Best Trick and High Jump challenges, the latter being the source of the most recent official Guinness World Records attempts (see below).

XPOGO

MOST BALLOONS POPPED USING A POGO STICK IN ONE MINUTE

One of our most pop-ular record-breakers is Britain's Mark Aldridge, who used his pogo stick to burst 57 balloons on April Fool's Day 2010. But this was no prank—Mark was appearing on Italian TV attempting successfully to pop his own record, which he beat by one balloon.

1920

The year in which a "spring and hopping stilt" was patented in Germany by Hans Pohlig and Ernst Gottschall. It's thought that this was the origin of the toy's name: **Po**hlig and **Go**ttschall.

HIGHEST JUMP ON A POGO STICK

Two people share the pogo high-jump record, which is based on clearing a horizontal bar. American pogo-stickers Biff Hutchison (left) and Dalton Smith (right) both cleared 10 ft 6 in (3.2 m) during Pogopalooza 2015 at WaWa Welcomes America in Philadelphia, Pennsylvania, on July 3, 2015. It's no surprise that these two are head and shoulders above the competition—Dalton is the world's highest-ranked pogo athlete, and Biff is #4.

TOYS

TOYS TO LIFE

THE NEXT GENERATION OF ACTION FIGURES

LARGEST SKYLANDER

As of August 2013, the largest Skylander was a "life-size" statue of Tree Rex standing 10 ft 4 in (3.15 m) tall. The rex-cellent reconstruction was carved from polystyrene by UK model company Sculpture Studios and is an exact scale duplicate of the Skylanders Giants figure, right down to the eyes that light up.

HIGHEST-ALTITUDE GAMING SESSION IN FREEFALL

As part of the European launch of *Skylanders: Trap Team* on October 10, 2014, publisher Activision hired a group of skydivers—the "Skytrappers"—to play the game while in freefall. At an altitude of 12,500 ft (3,810 m), the "Skytrappers" really put the "sky" into *Skylanders*!

WOW!

BEST-SELLING INTERACTIVE GAMING TOYS

More than 240 million Skylanders figures had been sold by February 2015, according to maker Activision. Based on research from Euromonitor International, Skylanders is also the **largest video game hardware accessory brand**, outselling rivals including Disney Infinity and Nintendo amiibo, as well as gaming devices such as Microsoft Kinect, earning $541.2 million in 2014.

FIRST VIDEO GAME COMPATIBLE WITH NINTENDO AMIIBO FIGURINES

First launched on November 21, 2014, amiibo figurines are a set of interactive toys modeled on the superstars of Nintendo. The amiibo connect wirelessly to the 3DS and Wii U, and the first game to work with the figures was *Super Smash Bros. for Wii U.* Twelve figurines were released in the first wave, including Mario, Donkey Kong, Kirby, and Link (pictured above, left to right).

NEAR-FIELD TECH

Interactive-toy gaming makes use of technology known as "near-field communication" (NFC). But how does it work?

NFC enables devices such as smartphones and contactless credit cards to "talk" to each other using radio signals. Data is swapped between devices by bringing one close to the other or tapping them together.

This "tap-and-go" concept uses tiny chips that run on very little power. When two of these chips are brought together, they form a wireless link that allows data to flow across the radio waves between the two devices.

NFC was introduced to gaming with Skylanders (see left), and LEGO® is the latest to join in the fun with its action-adventure game *LEGO Dimensions* (2015, pictured below).

FIRST INTERACTIVE TOYS BASED ON COMIC-BOOK CHARACTERS

Disney Infinity: Marvel Super Heroes, released in September 2014, is the first interactive-toy video game to incorporate characters from the comic-book universe. It includes familiar faces such as Spider-Man (left), The Avengers (below), and Groot and Rocket Raccoon from *Guardians of the Galaxy*, as well as supervillains such as Loki and the Green Goblin.

TRANSFORMERS

RECORD-BREAKING ROBOTS IN DISGUISE

3-IN-1
Supersize Transformers figure Metroplex (left) comes in three different configurations (shown below): the original robot, a battleship vehicle, and an entire city.

WOW!

LARGEST TRANSFORMERS TOY
First released in 2013, the Titan-class Metroplex is billed by Hasbro, the maker of the long-running toy line, as the largest Autobot ever sold. Standing 24 in (60.9 cm) tall in robot form (left), it surpasses the previous record holder—Fortress Maximus, released in 1987—by 2 in (5 cm). Also equipped with glowing eyes, Metroplex is enough to give even Megatron nightmares!

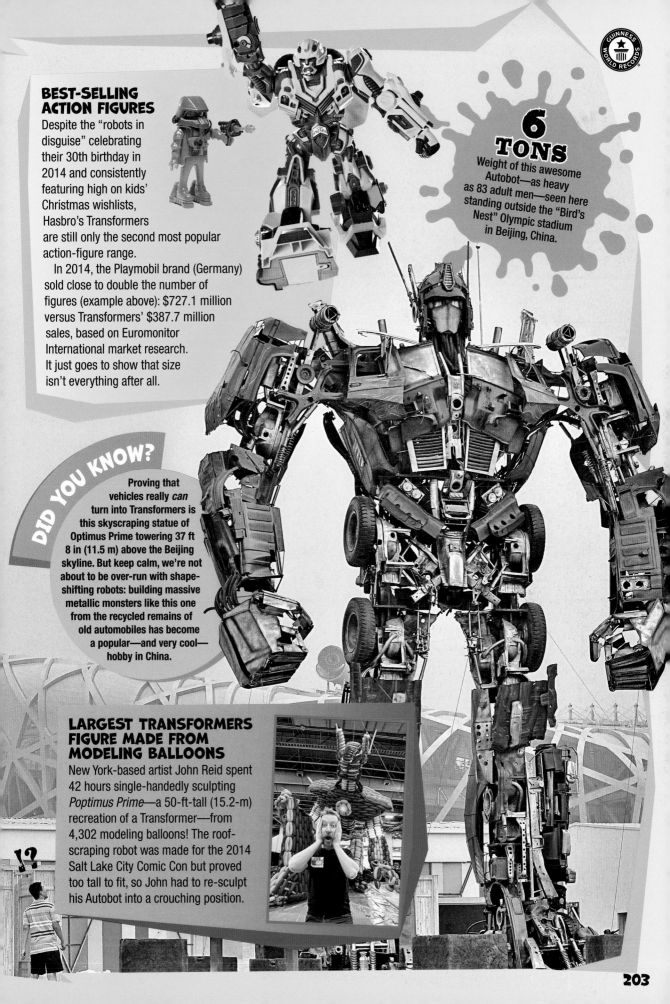

BEST-SELLING ACTION FIGURES

Despite the "robots in disguise" celebrating their 30th birthday in 2014 and consistently featuring high on kids' Christmas wishlists, Hasbro's Transformers are still only the second most popular action-figure range.

In 2014, the Playmobil brand (Germany) sold close to double the number of figures (example above): $727.1 million versus Transformers' $387.7 million sales, based on Euromonitor International market research. It just goes to show that size isn't everything after all.

6 TONS

Weight of this awesome Autobot—as heavy as 83 adult men—seen here standing outside the "Bird's Nest" Olympic stadium in Beijing, China.

DID YOU KNOW?

Proving that vehicles really *can* turn into Transformers is this skyscraping statue of Optimus Prime towering 37 ft 8 in (11.5 m) above the Beijing skyline. But keep calm, we're not about to be over-run with shape-shifting robots: building massive metallic monsters like this one from the recycled remains of old automobiles has become a popular—and very cool—hobby in China.

LARGEST TRANSFORMERS FIGURE MADE FROM MODELING BALLOONS

New York-based artist John Reid spent 42 hours single-handedly sculpting *Poptimus Prime*—a 50-ft-tall (15.2-m) recreation of a Transformer—from 4,302 modeling balloons! The roof-scraping robot was made for the 2014 Salt Lake City Comic Con but proved too tall to fit, so John had to re-sculpt his Autobot into a crouching position.

TOYS TOP 10
TOY BRANDS AT THE MOVIES

1 TRANSFORMERS
$3,778,297,170

With four live-action movies between 2007 and 2014, and an animation from 1986, the "robots in disguise" top our chart of the most successful toy lines at the international box office. The live-action films occupy four of the top five positions in the chart of single highest-grossing toy adaptations, with *Dark of the Moon* (2011) at number one, having earned $1.1 billion!

2 G.I. JOE
$674,392,077

"America's Movable Fighting Man" debuted in 1964, but it was 45 years later, with 2009's *G.I. Joe: The Rise of Cobra*, that the world's most famous action figure made it on to the big screen. A successful sequel in 2013 secured his place in the top 10.

3 LEGO®
$457,729,388

In its first foray into motion pictures, LEGO struck gold with the adventures of construction worker Emmet Brickowski. It's the fourth-highest-grossing single toy movie, behind three *Transformers* films. A sequel is under construction and is slated for 2018.

4 BATTLESHIP
$305,218,228

Hasbro's classic naval strategy game was transformed on the big screen in 2012 into a battle between the US Navy and an invading alien race. As unconnected as it was from the board game, it was obviously a winning strategy—and gave pop star Rihanna her first movie role.

5 CARE BEARS
$33,069,947

The cute line of teddy bear characters made their first appearance as plush toys in 1983, and within two years they were movie stars. The three *Care Bears* films for which there are figures were successful enough to secure the Bears' place in our top 10.

6 BRATZ
$25,747,223

The original Bratz fashion dolls Cloe, Jade, Sasha, and Yasmin first strutted their stuff in 2001. Following a popular TV series, their big-screen debut came in 2007. The plot followed four girls, played by human actors, starting at high school and showed how true friendship can overcome the culture of cliques.

7 AMERICAN GIRL
$17,657,973

The 18-in-tall (46-cm) American Girl dolls—sold alongside books by Valerie Tripp—have inspired various TV and direct-to-DVD movies. The most successful was 2008's *Kit Kittredge: An American Girl*, which received a theatrical release.

8 MASTERS OF THE UNIVERSE
$16,316,460

"Masters of the Universe" is the sword-and-sorcery toy line that features the muscle-bound He-Man and his arch foe, Skeletor. It got the live-action treatment in 1987, starring Dolph Lundgren as the hench hero.

9 MY LITTLE PONY
$5,958,456

While the 1986 animation *My Little Pony: The Movie* earned less than $6 million at the box office, the toy brand remains internationally celebrated. There have been more than 45 variants of Blossom (below), one of the six original ponies.

10 RAINBOW BRITE
$4,889,971

Like the American Girl and Care Bears franchises, Rainbow Brite was a toy line developed alongside a range of greetings cards. And like *My Little Pony*, the 1985 movie version underperformed at the box office— yet it still made it to no. 10 in the toy-movie chart!

BLOCKBUSTERS QUIZ

CHECK YOUR ANSWERS ON P. 209!

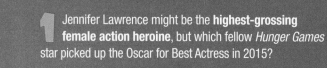

MOVIES

1 Jennifer Lawrence might be the **highest-grossing female action heroine**, but which fellow *Hunger Games* star picked up the Oscar for Best Actress in 2015?

2 As well as *Avengers: Age of Ultron* and *Ant-Man*, the world's **largest comic-book publisher**, Marvel, also released a rebooted *Fantastic Four* movie in 2015. What nickname does its protagonist Johnny Storm go by?

3 The much-anticipated *Star Wars: The Force Awakens* hit movie theaters late in 2015, but how many *Star Wars* movies have there been in total?

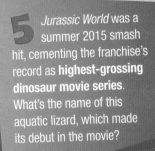

4 SpongeBob and co. ventured ashore in their summer blockbuster *Sponge Out of Water*. What's the name of their enemy in the movie, voiced by Antonio Banderas?

5 *Jurassic World* was a summer 2015 smash hit, cementing the franchise's record as **highest-grossing dinosaur movie series**. What's the name of this aquatic lizard, which made its debut in the movie?

1 In 2015, Elon Musk became one of *The Simpsons'* record-breaking total of 688 guest stars. In real life, what is the name of Musk's rocket-building company?

2 Mouse-type Pokémon Pikachu is the iconic face of the **longest-running video-game TV spinoff**. Name one more Mouse-type Pokémon.

3 Which *America's Got Talent* judge announced that 2015 would be their last season on the show? They currently hold the record for **highest-earning radio host** …

4 *Be Cool, Scooby-Doo!* on Boomerang is the 12th series to feature the ever-hungry Great Dane and the Mystery Incorporated gang. What's the name of Scooby's owner and best friend?

5 Peter Capaldi is the current Doctor in the **longest-running sci-fi show**, but how many actors have played Doctor Who, as of 2015?

COMICS & BOOKS

1 What was the title of the third book in the *Diary of a Wimpy Kid* series—the **most printed fictional children's diaries**?

2 In 2014, *Diary of a Wimpy Kid* creator Jeff Kinney was tied with Veronica Roth as **highest-earning children's author**. What is the name of the main character in Roth's *Divergent* trilogy?

3 *Guardians of the Galaxy* was the **highest-grossing comic-book adaptation movie** of 2014. What's the name of the tree character?

4 What is the number of the platform from which Harry Potter and his friends catch the *Hogwarts Express* in the **best-selling kids' book series ever**?

5 Perry White, Martha Kent, and Lex Luthor are characters from which famous comic-book series, featuring the **first superhero with superpowers**?

MUSIC

1 One Direction was the **first British band to reach No. 1 in the USA with their debut album**, in 2012. Which member of the group quit in March 2015?

2 Which Ed Sheeran and Pharrell Williams single appears on the tracklist for *Guitar Hero Live*, set for release in October 2015?

3 Katy Perry became the third singer to enter the 1-billion-view club for a music video with her song "Dark Horse." PSY's "Gangnam Style" was the first to achieve this feat, but which Canadian musician was the second?

5 Selena Gomez's victory at the 2015 Nickelodeon Kids' Choice Awards means that she has won the **most Favorite Female Singer awards**. Fellow musicians Jessie J, Ariana Grande, and Nicki Minaj picked up the Favorite Song award, but for which catchy tune?

4 Holder of the record for **fastest-selling digital single**, Taylor Swift smashed through the 5-million sales mark in the USA for her album *1989* in July 2015. It was her third album to achieve this. Can you name either of the other two?

TECH

1 What is the most popular operating system for smartphones and tablets?

2 The world's **largest company by market value**, Apple, released its long-anticipated smartwatch in 2015. What name did they give it?

3 We are now on the eighth generation of games consoles, but what is the **best-selling games console** ever?

4 Atlas may be the **most agile humanoid robot**, but it's not the fastest runner. That accolade goes to ASIMO. From which country does this droid hail?

5 The *New Horizons* probe set the record for the **fastest Earth departure**, speeding away from our planet at an eye-watering 36,250 mph (58,338 km/h)! Which dwarf planet did the probe approach in 2015?

TOYS

1 In 2015, the world's **largest construction toy brand** launched *LEGO® Dimensions*. The initial toys-to-life line was due to include Batman, Wyldstyle, and which famous wizard from Middle Earth?

2 Dracula might be the **most portrayed literary character in movies**, but in the popular doll range and TV series *Monster High*, his daughter, Draculaura, gets a starring role. Can you name one of the other five Original Ghouls from the series?

3 The **largest remote-control toy brand**, Air Hogs, makes all kinds of helicopters and mini-drones. What do you call a helicopter with four rotors?

4 As well as its foam-bullet blasters, the **best-selling outdoor toy brand**, NERF, is also famous for its water pistols. What's the name of this line?

5 A lot of people use these multicolored rubber bands to make jewelry. What are they better known as?

APPS & ONLINE

1 In the default settings of the popular video-messaging app Snapchat, what is the maximum time that viewers can see their Snaps before they disappear?

2 Portuguese soccer star Cristiano Ronaldo is the current king of Facebook with more "likes" than anyone else. For which Spanish soccer club does he play?

3 Marzia Bisognin, the girlfriend of YouTube's **most subscribed star** "PewDiePie," is a vlogging sensation in her own right. What nickname is she better known by?

4 The world's **most used search engine** Google took its name from a large number known as a "googol." How many zeroes after a "1" does a googol have?

5 *Minecraft: Pocket Edition* is the **best-selling iOS app**. Can you identify these three mods from the game? (One point for each.)

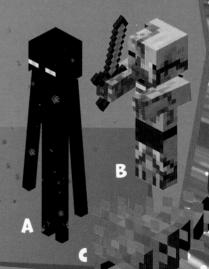

ANSWERS

INDEX

INDEX

PICTURE CREDITS

2/3 Mojang, Instagram, Warner Bros./LEGO/Games Press, Getty Images/Disney

4/5 Alamy, Walt Disney Pictures, Activision, Warner Bros./LEGO, Universal Pictures, Lucasfilm, Mojang, Marvel, Supercell, Nickelodeon, Activision/Marvel

6/7 Sonja Horsman/Guinness World Records

8/9 Disney/Alamy, Universal Pictures, DreamWorks/Alamy, Lucasfilm, Pixar Animation Studios, Universal Pictures

10/11 Universal/Alamy, Disney/Alamy, Disney/Imagenet, Warner Bros./Rex Features

12/13 Alamy, Disney/Alamy, Walt Disney Animation Studios, Reuters

14/15 Getty Images, Dr Cox/National Physical Laboratory

16/17 Lucasfilm, Lucasfilm animation, Lucasfilm/Alamy, Alamy, Reuters

18/19 EA, TT Games, Mojang, Mashable

20/21 Ryan Schude/Guinness World Records

22/23 New Line Cinema/Alamy, Turbine, Ranald Mackechnie/Guinness World Records, EA

24/25 Universal/Kobal, Universal/Alamy, Alamy

26/27 Alamy, Canadian Press/REX

28/29 Everett/REX Shutterstock, Reuters, Kevin Scott Ramos/Guinness World Records, Alamy

30/31 Glenn Murphy

32/33 Marvel/20th Century Fox/Alamy, Reuters/Jim Ruymen, European Southern Observatory, Marvel/Nokia

34/35 Sonja Horsman/Guinness World Records, Universal

36/37 DreamWorks/Alamy, James Ellerker/Guinness World Records, Pathe/DreamWorks/Aardman/Alamy

38/39 Studio Ghibli/Alamy, Alamy

40/41 Disney/Alamy, James Ellerker/Guinness World Records, Ubisoft/Games Press

42/43 Alamy, Disney/Alamy, Disney/Games Press, Disney/Pixar

44/45 Disney, Disney/Pixar/Alamy, Disney/Alamy, Universal/Alamy, DreamWorks/Alamy, 20th Century Fox/Alamy

46/47 20th Century Fox/Alamy, Universal, Marvel/Paramount/Imagenet, Universal, Marvel/Imagenet, Warner Bros./Alamy, New Line/Alamy, Paramount/Alamy

48/49 Scholastic/Alamy, Alamy, Abrams Books, Scholastic

50/51 Alamy, Paul Michael Hughes/Guinness World Records

52/53 Ryan Schude/Guinness World Records

54/55 Sonja Horsman/Guinness World Records

56/57 Alamy, Atari/Wiki, Warner Bros./Alamy, Rex Features

58/59 Activision/Games Press, Alamy, Columbia/Alamy, Reuters

60/61 Warner Bros., Kevin Scott Ramos/Guinness World Records, Jana DeHart, Warner Bros./Games Press, Alamy, Heritage Auctions, DC Comics/Alamy

62/63 Corbis, Alamy, PA, Warner Bros./Alamy

64/65 Alamy

66/67 Columbia Pictures/Picselect, Scholastic, Dan Nelken/Scholastic, Columbia Pictures/Picselect, Universal/Alamy, Summit Entertainment/Alamy, Hachette Book Group

68/69 20th Century Fox/Alamy, Royal Geographical Society/Alamy, Jeff Kinney/Twitter, Abrams Books

70/71 Lionsgate/Alamy, Scholastic/Alamy, Ryan Schude/Guinness World Records, Alamy

72/73 Paul Michael Hughes/Guinness World Records, Richard Bradbury/Guinness World Records, Paul Michael Hughes/Guinness World Records, Drew Gardner/Guinness World Records

74/75 Random House, 20th Century Fox, Scholastic, Harper Collins, Little, Brown, Disney Publishing, HMH Books, Abrams Books, St Martin's Press, Harper Collins, Aladdin/Simon & Schuster

76/77 Steve Marsel Studio/Nervous System, Samsung, Nintendo, Alamy, Boston Dynamics/Alamy, Google, Reuters, Raspberry Pi Foundation

78/79 Samsung, Alamy, www.nordicfactory.com

80/81 Nintendo, Google, Alamy, www.nordicfactory.com, Reuters

82/83 Katia Vega, Alamy, Fitbit, Lechal, WeeX, Immerz, Pebble

84/85 Reuters, Computer History Museum, PA, Getty Images, Alamy, Elysium Partners

86/87 NASA/Wiki, Resin.io, Raspberry Pi Foundation

88/89 Alamy, Wiki, Grupo Sicnova, Steve Marsel Studio/Nervous System, Freedom of Creation, MiS/NASA, Frank Wojciechowski

90/91 Nicolas Halftermeyer/Wiki, Mohammed Bin Rashid Space Centre, Alamy, Pix4D, Reuters

92/93 Sonja Horsman/Guinness World Records, NASA, Derek Eckenroth/Bob Jones University

94/95 Boston Dynamics/Alamy, Boston Dynamics/Reuters, Reuters

96/97 Reuters, Alamy, PA, Universita Campus Bio-Medica di Roma/Flickr

98/99 Richard Bradbury/Guinness World Records

100/101 Sony, Nintendo, Nintendo/Alamy, Sony/Alamy, Microsoft, Nintendo/Wiki, Shutterstock

102/103 Reuters, Ryan Schude/Guinness World Records, Reuters, Paul Michael Hughes/Guinness World Records, Ranald Mackechnie/Guinness World Records

104/105 Reuters, Big Machine Records, Kevin Scott Ramos/Guinness World Records

106/107 Alamy, Epic Records/Alamy, Reuters, Atlantic Records

108/109 Reuters, Alamy

110/111 Richard Bradbury/Guinness World Records, James Ellerker/Guinness World Records, Drew Gardner/Guinness World Records

112/113 Paul Michael Hughes/Guinness World Records, Carr and Craighead/Cornell, Ryan Schude/Guinness World Records

114/115 Sonja Horsman/Guinness World Records, Activision/Games Press

116/117 Chris Hadfield © Canadian Space Agency, 2013, NASA, AP Photo/Paul McCartney, Bill Bernstein

118/119 Alamy, Reuters, Jaroslaw Nogal, Jacek Waszkiewicz

120/121 Ryan Schude/Guinness World Records, Paul Michael Hughes/Guinness World Records, Shinsuke Kamioka/Guinness World Records, Ranald Mackechnie/Guinness World Records

122/123 Alamy, Singstar.com

124/125 Reuters, Alamy

126/127 Henson Prod./Reuters, Disney/Alamy, Hanna-Barbera/Alamy, 20th Century Fox/Rex Features, Fox Kids/Alamy, Nickelodeon/Picselect, Bonhams

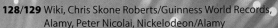

128/129 Wiki, Chris Skone Roberts/Guinness World Records, Alamy, Peter Nicolai, Nickelodeon/Alamy

130/131 Sonja Horsman/Guinness World Records, Nickelodeon

132/133 Paramount/REX, Alamy, Ryan Schude/ Guinness World Records, Ubisoft/Games Press

134/135 North Shore News/Cindy Goodman, Drew Gardner/ Guinness World Records, Kevin Scott Ramos/ Guinness World Records, Alamy, Hanna-Barbera/ Alamy, Warner/Mosaic/Alamy

136/137 TM & © 2015 SCG Power Rangers LLC. All Rights Reserved

138/139 Rex Features, Alamy, Hanna-Barbera/Alamy

140/141 Henson Prod./Alamy, Hasbro/PA, Alamy, Henson/ Alamy

142/143 20th Century Fox/Alamy, Alamy

144/145 Ranald Mackechnie/Guinness World Records, Valerie Blum, Alamy, 20th Century Fox/Alamy, 20th Century Fox/Rex Features

146/147 BBC/PA Images, Richard Bradbury/Guinness World Records, Bonhams, Ranald Mackechnie/Guinness World Records

148/149 20th Century Fox/Alamy, Warner Bros./Alamy, PBS/ Marc Brown, Nickelodeon, Nickelodeon/Imagenet, Nickelodeon/Alamy, Hanna-Barbera/Alamy, Lucasfilm/Alamy

150/151 Rovio, Google, YouTube/Alamy, Alamy, Mojang, Supercell, Instagram, Twitter/Alamy, Facebook

152/153 Alamy, Outfit7, Supercell, Columbia Pictures/Rovio/ Picselect, Rovio

154/155 Alamy, Songkick, NGA/iTunes, Google/Alamy, Universal/YouTube, Spotify/iTunes, CEMAS, Brad Reynolds, TripAdvisor/iTunes, Reuters

156/157 Kickstarter, M3D, Amanda Palmer, Jake Bronstein, Zachery Weiner, Rich Burlew, Alamy, Ys Net

158/159 Alamy, Daniel Deme/Guinness World Records, Paul Michael Hughes/Guinness World Records, James Ellerker/Guinness World Records, LEGO, Mojang

160/161 Gaermine/YouTube, GNRfrancis/YouTube, MCMagic, Ragnur Le Barbare/PlanetMinecraft, FVDisco/ YouTube, WesterosCraft

162/163 King Digital/Games Press; Reuters; Ranald Mackechnie/ Guinness World Records; Fran Morales/Guinness World Records; Gary He/Insider Images for M&M's

164/165 Sonja Horsman/Guinness World Records, Alamy

166/167 Reuters, Twitter/Alamy, Alamy

168/169 Interscope/Shady, Reuters, Alamy, Kendall Jenner/ Instagram, Alamy, Shakira/Twitter, Sony Music

170/171 Guinness World Records/YouTube, PSY/YG Entertainment/YouTube, Red Bull/YouTube, Lucasfilm/Imagenet, Reuters, Tom Cassell/Syndicate, Alamy

172/173 Blucollection/YouTube, DisneyCarToys/YouTube, TheEducVideos/YouTube, DisneyCollectorBR/ YouTube, Alamy, PewDiePie/YouTube, LittleBabyBum/YouTube, PopularMMOs/ YouTube, Alamy

174/175 Google, Alamy, Reuters, Paragon and Dave Jourdan, Google, JAXA/YouTube

176/177 Kim Kardashian/Instagram, Beyoncé/Instagram, Taylor Swift/Instagram, Selena Gomez/Instagram, Ariana Grande/Instagram, Justin Bieber/Instagram, Kendall Jenner/Instagram, Kylie Jenner/Instagram, Nicki Minaj/Instagram, Khloé Kardashian/Instagram, Instagram

178/179 Alamy, Ranald Mackechnie/Guinness World Records, Disney Interactive/Marvel/Games Press, Warner Bros./LEGO/Games Press, Nick Gillott, Alamy

180/181 Sonja Horsman/Guinness World Records, Alamy

182/183 Nick Gillott, Bloodhound SSC

184/185 Cristian Barnett/Guinness World Records

186/187 Warner Bros./LEGO/Games Press, LucasArts/ LEGO/Games Press, Warner Bros./LEGO/Marvel/ Games Press

188/189 Sonja Horsman/Guinness World Records

190/191 Ryan Schude/Guinness World Records, Nintendo/ Games Press, Paul Michael Hughes/Guinness World Records

192/193 Warner Bros./Alamy, Nintendo/Games Press

198/199 James Ellerker/Guinness World Records, James Roumeliotis, Ranald Mackechnie/Guinness World Records, Pogopalooza, Alamy

200/201 Aden Hynes, Activision, Nintendo, Warner Bros./ LEGO/Games Press, Activision/Games Press, Disney Interactive/Marvel/Games Press

202/203 Hasbro, Alamy

204/205 Paramount/Alamy, Alamy, Warner Bros./Alamy, Universal/Alamy, Lionsgate/Alamy, New Line/ Alamy, Cannon Films/Alamy, Mattel/Alamy, Hasbro/ Sunbow/Ronald Grant

206/207 20th Century Fox/Marvel/Picselect, Nickelodeon/ Alamy, Alamy, Warner Bros./Alamy, Summit Entertainment/Alamy, Marvel Studios/Alamy

208/209 Alamy, Asylum Records/YouTube, Reuters, Apple, NASA/APL/SwRI, Snapchat, Mojang

210/211 Reuters, Rovio

212/213 Pixar Animation Studios, 20th Century Fox/ Rex Features, Bonhams

214/215 Nickelodeon/Picselect, Universal Pictures

216 Shinsuke Kamioka/Guinness World Records, James Ellerker/Guinness World Records, Ranald Mackechnie/Guinness World Records

Guinness World Records would like to thank the following for their help with the making of *Guinness World Records Blockbusters 2016*: Activision (Rachael Grant and Jonathan Fargher), Mark Aston, Russell Barnes, Jane Crawford, Barney Curnow, Toby Curnow, Toby Ewen, Dora Howard, Charlie Howell, Res Kahraman, Rohan Mehra, Rovio (Karyn Castillo), Matthew White, Robert Zwetsloot

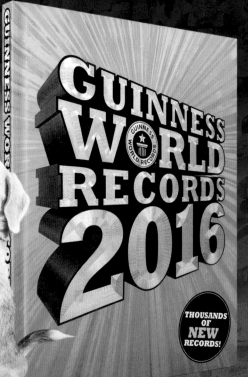